Talking out of School

Library of Congress Cataloging-in-Publication Data

Fleisher, Kass, 1959-
Talking out of school / Kass Fleisher. -- 1st ed.
     p. cm.
ISBN 978-1-56478-517-6 (pbk. : alk. paper)
1. Fleisher, Kass, 1959- 2. English teachers--United
States--Biography. 3. Women college teachers--United
States--Biography. 4. Women in higher education--United States. 5.
Sexism in higher education--United States. 6. Racism in
education--United States. I. Title.
PE64.F58A3 2008
378.1'2092--dc22
[B]
                                   2008014614

Grateful acknowledgement is made to the editors of New Ohio Review (nor),
who published a section of this work.

Partially funded by a grant from the Illinois Arts Council, a state agency,
and by the University of Illinois at Urbana-Champaign

www.dalkeyarchive.com

Cover art: Burden of Memory, oil, by Maria Tomasula. Used by permission.

Printed on permanent/durable acid-free paper
and bound in the United States of America

Talking out of School
memoir of an educated woman

by Kass Fleisher

Dalkey Archive Press Champaign & London

Contents

for all who taught me
especially
Joe

Let the woman learne in silence
with all subiection.
But I suffer not a woman to teach, nor
to vsurpe authoritie ouer the
man, but to be in silence.

1611 King James translation
of I Timothie ii, 11-12
Attributed to Paul

This sentence has hope as origin.

How to Write, 1931
Gertrude Stein

Threads

1.

The first teacher I ever met caught me in perhaps the most unflattering moment of my life—slimy, blood-streaked, bruised, and shrieking. A desiccating tube streams from belly to knees. I can neither walk nor crawl, let alone stand up to take my licks. In the early moments of my life a worker does her best to clean me up, make me presentable, get some clothes on me—and hand me over to the teacher, where I lie, for eternity, on her collapsed belly.

———

Light snapped on, covers stripped back, arm jerked.
   "Get up! Get up!"

"Huh?" Ripped out of bed at god knows when in the morning. She's next door in my brother's room now. "Get up! Get up!"

"Huh?"

"Get downstairs!"

"What's going on?"

"Both of you, get downstairs!"

Socks on wood steps—we tumble down six to the landing by the bathroom. She's got us each by one arm, yanks us to the bathroom door.

"Who touched this?"

"Huh?"

"Stop saying 'Huh' after everything I say! Who *touched* this?"

We follow her finger to the doorknob, from which dangles, by one strap, a bra.

"What?" I say.

"Don't be obtuse. You know what I'm asking you. *Who touched this!*"

"What makes you think someone *touched* it?"

I'm living dangerous: I've put on my are-you-fucking-nuts? voice.

"Because I left it in a certain spot, and I can tell it's been moved. So who moved it?"

I stare at her.

SMACK. In the kisser. Wipes that eye-roll right out from under my brow.

But she has to let go of my arm to do it. I'm out of reach against a wall before she can say "brat."

"I'm going to ask you one last time. *Who moved this!*"

I stare at her.

She rips at my brother's arm. His small limb is red now, chafed. "You did it, didn't you," she says. "You moved it."

"No."

"I know it was you. How many times have I told you not to touch my stuff!" With her now-free hand she wallops my brother on his butt.

"Nobody touched your goddamn *bra*," I say. "It's right where you goddamn left it."

It probably comes out with something of a sneer attached. She releases my brother, who skids across the landing in his socks, crashing into a closet door. We're each glued to opposite walls in an effort to stay beyond her reach.

"I am *sick* of *kids* who don't respect my *things*," she says, matching me sneer for sneer and taking a step closer to me for emphasis. Now she's in my face. "And *you*—"

she grabs a chunk of my long hair and *yanks*—

"should *know*—"

yank—

"what I *expect*—"

kicks *shins*—

"when I'm *gone*."

shins.

"Get back up to bed."

Toe jabs follow us up the stairs but most of them miss us. I collapse on the other side of my door.

"DOORS OPEN!" she yells. "Don't make me come up there again!"

I bang it open. In my head I'm screaming.

BITCH!

When my brother wakes up the next morning, his head is stuck to his pillow.

———

But this isn't how my brother remembers it. He recollects us being locked in the bathroom and told we couldn't come out till we'd settled on a perpetrator.

When my brother wakes up the next morning, his head is stuck to his pillow.

———

"She thinks it's me," my brother recalls saying. "She always does. Let's just have it be me."

———

My first memory is either my father leaving or the Kennedy assassination: my mother sitting in front of the TV all day, crying.

———

My mother, brother and I move around a good bit, to places in the Philly area determined by my mother's marital and economic status. I start elementary school near our row home in Chester, a dicey town on its way to being the worst of dicey towns, where my single mother finds security in a German shepherd pup that grows quickly into a growl on four legs. Two elementary schools later we land here, in this far more distant suburb, one notch up from row homes. Our development, on the edge of town—out by the sewage plant—winds with four-plexes crammed together, housing working- and middle-class families. Kids race everywhere, and we all live in identical split-level houses. Through the front door is the living room; down six steps is the basement, which my grandfather has helped my mother carpet; up six steps is the dining room and kitchen; up six more is the bathroom and my mother's darkened bedroom; up the last six is my room and my brother's room.

I've got the room with the view of the alley and the soybean field out back.

Postage-stamp yards, all fenced.

My mother doesn't talk much to the neighbors. "I don't want anybody knowing my business," she says. "I don't want to be beholden to anyone."

Anyone who comes to our front door gets a faceful of very tall, very powerful German shepherd.

The walls are thin.

Next door, we hear Mr. and Mrs. Patrick fighting. Baritone bellowing is frequently followed by thumps. Their two girls spend a lot of time on our shared stoop. My brother considers one his girlfriend. At night the two of them invent their own Morse code, knock at each other through Sheetrock.

When we see her, Mrs. Patrick doesn't look well. My brother's girlfriend has an odd rash on her face.

I'm in my teens, an activist. I'm out, as they say, to change the world. I'm in the kitchen with a dustrag in one hand and Pledge in the other when my mother walks in. We hear bellows followed by thumps and train our eyes elsewhere. Shame mauls us both. It's embarrassment we feel for the Patricks, for their—no, it's her, just *her*—audible humiliation. *Him* I hate, openly. I don't speak to him when I see him. When I see Mrs. Patrick, I do something vague with my eyes, something that lets me perceive her figure, her disposition, but not her face.

"I think we should do something," I say.

"What do you mean?" my mother asks mildly.

"I think we should call somebody," I say. God knows where I picked this up—at school, maybe, or reading. "The cops, or social workers, somebody."

My mother seems to consider it. "No," she says finally.

"Why not?" I say. My brows squish together.

"You just don't know about people," she says. She speaks almost sorrowfully. "It could make things worse."

I turn and face her. "How?"

She walks away from me. I've been dusting the top of the aquarium. She's wiping down counters. "People have problems. You just don't know what's going on over there."

"I hear it. I see it."

"You just don't know," she says. "We're better off staying out of it."

———

I ask my father one time why his marriage to my mother didn't work out. He rolls up his forehead as if it were an impossible question.

"I think she had English teacher's disease," he says.

"What's that?"

"It was like she'd come home and not realize it wasn't three o'clock anymore. She wasn't at the head of the class anymore. She wasn't the boss of everything."

"Oh," I say. "Yeah."

———

I'm in eighth grade, junior high school, friends with Clare, who to me is exotic because she and her mother live in an apartment complex with a pool. Clare and I splash around with zero supervision or provisions, her mother off working all hours. I find Clare just as exotic as my other friend, Marie, who lives in a big house in the country, her mother hovering over every second of my visits, using cookies, cake, candy, any kind of simple carbohydrate as an excuse to enter the room.

I love that cookies and candy are unregulated there, and that cake actually exists. I also love hootin' and hollerin' and closing Clare's bedroom door and lying on her bed watching all manner of TV without someone up my ass about where or what or how I should be.

My friends never come to my house.

Thanks to my mother, my brain comes equipped with extraordinary radar, with which I can locate disapproval anywhere within one-hundred miles. I receive crystal-clear communications from these mothers about their daughters and me. Cookies or no, Marie's mother doesn't like me. Marie tells me her mother says I'm too "worldly." Turns out they're Jehovah's Witnesses, whatever that means. Across town, though, Clare's mother is entirely indifferent to the matter.

Marie and Clare don't like each other.

Somehow, I tell Clare what's going on at home. Not Marie, or if I tell Marie, there's no response.

"That's nuts," Clare says.

I don't quite fathom this.

We're in Clare's room, thinking about how hungry we are, waiting for Clare's mother, who's stopping for hoagies on her way home.

"Your mother's fucking crazy," Clare says.

I don't quite fathom this. I'm used to thinking it's my fault.

"No way," Clare says. "People shouldn't be allowed to fucking coldcock people just because they're having a bad fucking day."

I don't quite fathom this. I'm used to thinking it's my fault. My brother is the crazy one in the family. This is clear from the frequency with which my mother hauls him to shrinks. The last shrink diagnosed him as a borderline psychopath.

"You gotta talk to somebody," Clare says. "It could get bad for you in there."

Borderline psychopath, my mother says.

Clare's mother comes home with the fat sandwiches rolled up in butcher paper. We unfurl them across the small kitchen table, razor-thin onion slices flying in all directions. In a flash I'm on the floor, picking them up.

"Let it go," Clare's mother says. "Let it go, really. Easier to get all at once later."

Psychopath, my mother says. You believe that?

I have to look the word up.

"Thank you for the hoagie, Mrs. Connor," I say.

"We were famished," Clare says. She gets her jaws around a chunk of misbehaving cold cuts, and yanks. "Ou ould ell her," she says, looking at me.

"What?" I say.

Clare swallows the cold cuts all but whole, prosciutt' hanging off her bottom lip. "You should tell her," she says. She jerks her head toward her mother.

"What?" I giggle a bit. It's a bit-giggle, a through-the-teeth gesture, high in the throat, cheekbones lifted. My braces peek out.

"Tell her."

I giggle.

"She's got this mother," Clare says, "nuts, out of her mind, pissed off permanently. Beats her up all the fucking time. Yelling, hollering, crazy."

I giggle.

"Geez," Mrs. Connor says. "My dad was like that."

I chew on a bit of hoagie.

"She's gotta talk to somebody," Clare says.

"Yeah," Mrs. Connor says. "You should."

I giggle.

"You should, really," Clare says.

"Who would I talk to?" I say through lifted cheekbones.

"Who would she talk to?" Clare asks her mother.

"I don't know," Mrs. Connor says. "You don't want to call the cops."

I burst out laughing.

"Aren't there social workers or something?" Clare says. She pops a tomato slice into her wide-opened mouth.

"There's guidance counselors I guess," Mrs. Connor says.

Psychopath, my mother says. Know what that means? she says. That means he has no conscience. He just acts. He doesn't think about the consequences because he doesn't care about the consequences.

I make the appointment. I have to bring a note to get out of my gym class to go see her.

I sit outside her office, my stomach grasped, strangled.

She calls me in. All of the furniture is wood. It's a bright office, with a window facing a nearby park, Memorial Park, a place of grass, trees, iron castings of cannons, and a bronze statue of some guy. I never ask who he is, though I've been by countless times, waiting in the car as my mother runs into her classroom after hours. My mother used to teach in this building. It used to be the high school. It became a junior high only a year ago, when the high school was moved to a huge complex outside of town. The other two junior highs were reorganized, and my new student body was cobbled together from several neighborhoods. My friends from elementary school ended up somewhere else.

"What can I help you with today?" the guidance counselor says.

The cheekbones reach. The voice shrieks. The throat squeezes.

She listens soberly.

I touch my forehead, I grip my skull with two hands, I wave my palms in the air, I chortle.

She listens.

I laugh.

I conclude by saying that someone told me to come in and talk about it. With wild gesticulations I communicate that I don't really have the right to tell the tale. I really shouldn't be here. I don't actually need her help.

It emerges ironical. Eye-rolls. You-knows. Whatevers. I am the walking illustration of saying one thing and meaning another. That's why I'm so fucking amused. I'm performing panic and resilience at the same time.

But it's not irony—because this mode of communication communicates perplexity perfectly.

What's more laughable than the irresolute? They make hit TV shows out of this: door number one, door number two, door number three. Take your pick.

It's unanalyzable. I dress up like Raggedy Ann and hoot and holler and Monte picks me and offers me $200 for every toothpick I have in my purse. I don't have any but he gives me $200 anyway. Then he gives me a chance to choose my life, right there on national television. Door number one: I love my mother, I stay with my mother, I get crushed. Door number two: I hate my mother, I stay with my mother, *I hate my mother*. Door number three: the goat with the $200 gift certificate for a lifetime supply of toothpicks.

I have braces, so toothpicks aren't a half-bad idea.

That is to say, I have no fucking idea how to protect myself.

That is to say, the more I laugh, the harder I'm screaming.

She leans forward and puts her elbows on her desk. "What you might want to keep in mind," she says slowly, already decided, already drained of any real response, "is that your mother's probably having a rough time. You might want to try to see it from her perspective."

I stare at the floor, exhausted, no gestures left in the tank. My cheeks flame.

"She's a single mother. She works a hard job. She probably has money problems. From what you say, it sounds like your brother is hard to handle. And I see here that you missed almost four weeks of school last year. There's a note on your grade reports that says you have asthma. Are you sick a lot?"

I shrug. There's no carpet. Just linoleum in some irreconcilably alternating combination of grays. That gray speckles with this gray, then this gray speckles with this gray and some more of that gray. The color never evens out into a replicating pattern.

"Your mother has a lot on her plate." The woman is heavy in what strikes me as a maternal way, busty, low-voiced, kind. "Maybe it would help to remember that."

The cheeks sear.

I knew it was my fault. See? Told ya. I'm just not *understanding* enough.

My goose is cooked before I'm even home from school. My mother bangs open the front door early, shortly after three. My brother's not back from elementary school yet.

She slams her car keys into her pocketbook and tosses that onto the coffee table. Her coat lands on the couch.

"Get down here.

"How could you.

"Don't you understand, she's a *coworker* of mine.

"That's *work*. This is our *house*. What goes on in this *house* stays in this *house*.

"Do you understand me.

"I have to have some *privacy*. This is *private*, what you're talking about.

"I have to *work* with her."

Two years later, the year I move on to the high school where my mother works, the guidance counselor gets a new job. She'll be Vice Principal of our high school. She starts the same year I do. In fact, each of the Vice Principals is assigned a graduating class, and the new Vice Principal is assigned to mine.

Whenever I see her in the halls, my complexion slides into pink applesauce.

In January of my miserable, boring, excruciating senior year, my environmental science teacher hands me a note in lab. I'm to report to the Vice Principal's office.

My gut is there already. It's been yanked and twisted the whole way across our gigantic school. *How am I in trouble?* When I stumble into the outer office, another kid is there, a guy I know from chorus. In time a girl comes in, also in chorus. We're called into her inner office together. *OK, how am I in trouble with* these *geeks*?

Her new office is carpeted.

She gestures toward me and the guy. "I just wanted to call you both in to say that we know that both of you have been accepted Early Decision to attend _____ College. And Cindy here has won Early Acceptance."

The carpet is gray. No, it's brown. It's taupe. Right? Taupe? Isn't that both?

"It's a great honor for us to have exceptional students like you going on to such a good college. It helps the students who come after you, because it means we have a good working relationship with that school. They'll take others as seriously as they've taken you."

Early Acceptance. What's that?

"Congratulations."

I tear ass off the taupe carpet. If I never again have to confront that humiliating mistake from eighth grade, it'll be too soon.

Out in the corridor, I turn to Cindy. "What's Early Acceptance?" I ask.

"It's where you skip your senior year and go straight to college," she says.

FUCK. You can DO that? You mean, I coulda been outta this shithole a YEAR ago? I coulda been outta that fucking house A YEAR AGO?

Where's a good guidance counselor when you fucking NEED ONE?

CHRIST!

———

Here is all I will ever need to say about pedagogy:

When I'm a teen, my brother about eleven or so, I get off the extra-curricular bus, the bus they run for kids who stay after school and do cool stuff like work on the student paper, attend choral practice, organize Earth Day with the Environmental Action club—well, who knows what I was doing, but it was a bad fucking day. A bad fucking day. And there in the kitchen sits my little brother, doing his homework. I walk right the fuck up to him, wind up with everything I've got, and wallop him right in the upper arm. "Ow!" he screams, grabbing his arm. "What the hell did you do that for?"

But for me it's already over. I'm smiling. It feels great. I feel like a new woman. About his mortification I care not a whit.

"I'm telling Mom!" he yells.

"Grow up," I say. "Jesus. What a baby."

When I was six months old, or so the story was told, over and over, I turned blue and my mother in a terrible panic rushed me to the doctor to discover that I was asthmatic and terribly allergic to her cat. The family joke is that it was a horrible decision—keep the kid, or keep the cat? The cat went. So did the rugs, the draperies, and the stuffed animals.

"I had to clean every day," my mother says for the thousandth time. "I had to put up Venetian blinds—do you have any idea how hard it is to clean Venetian blinds? Every day I came home from school and dusted and vacuumed. Every day."

I'm about five when my mother presses a dustrag into my hands. "I've been cleaning for years," she says. "You're old enough to help now."

So it begins.

By the time I'm in junior high, I'm cleaning five days a week. On Mondays and Wednesdays after school I dust and vacuum the upstairs—my mother's room (which I tiptoe around, as if in a sacred sanctuary) and the dining room; on Tuesdays and Thursdays I do the downstairs—the living room and basement. On Wednesdays I wash clothes. On Sundays we go full-bore for two hours: I dust, my mother vacuums, I clean the bathrooms and kitchen, she washes sheets and clothes. Of course, this colossal campaign to beat back dust mites does help, since I'm also allergic to dogs. Of course, *not having a dog* would help even more, but never mind. "If I can't have a cat I'm having a dog," she says on at least forty-seven separate occasions. "That's all there is to it. You're not *that* allergic to him."

When he licks my skin I break out in bumps within minutes. If I touch him and then touch my eyes, my eyes itch for an hour straight.

"Kass! Get down here!"

I hover as far back from her as I can get away with.

"Was this here when you dusted it?"

She's pointing at a lamp on the end table. It's off-center.

"I guess not."

"You guess not. You guess right. It was here." She moves it. "Was *this* here?"

She's pointing at an ashtray.

Oh yeah, she smokes, too. Dog dander and smoke.

She points at a decorative plate made of thick green glass molded in the shape of a leaf sitting on the HiFi. She points at some candlesticks next to a bowl. She points at a bowl of fake red grapes on a treadle sewing machine near the front door.

"Get over here."

I take a step.

"I said get over here."

"*Here.*"

She lunges toward me—she's fast. In one movement she gets in my space and in my hair. She grasps a good fistful, which she tugs toward the coffee table. I follow along with. She jerks the hair down to the level of the table.

"Was this here?"

"No."

"No. Where was it?"

"In the middle."

"In the middle, very good. Put it there."

Bent double, and out from under the mass of hair, I reach a hand forward and give the fake red, orange, and yellow flowers a shove.

She lets go. I stand up and leap back.

"I don't think it's too much to ask you to put things back where they belong," she says. "You're grounded, one week."

"But I have majorette prac—"

"One week."

At school I'm a disgrace. "You're never not grounded," my friends bark. "What'd you do, rob a bank?"

That said, it's not like she doesn't have a point. When my mother's in the house I'm a one-teen-cleaning-machine, but when she's not, I find ways to escape what I tell my friends is chattel slavery. I read while I dust. I kneel, place the book on the end of the couch, shove stuff on the end table out of my way, read while I swipe cloth, move the stuff back, move the other stuff, read while I swipe cloth, move the stuff back. I get up, sit in the middle of the couch, put the book in my lap, move stuff on the coffee table out of the way, read/swipe, move, move, read/swipe, move.

There I sit for a few minutes, reading a full page, till I get up again, thinking I'll never get this done if I don't get moving . . .

I turn on the upright vacuum cleaner, push with right hand, hold book in left.

"Kass! Get down here!"

I can't maintain my ever-widening social space in the small bathroom. "You call this clean?" *SLAP* on the cheek. "Look at this. You didn't even *bother* to get under this rim." *KICK* in the shin. "What is wrong with you? You're *not* this careless about the things *you* care about. Look at this." *YANK* on the hair. "Get this clean, *now*." She throws a can of Dow bathroom cleaner at me; it hits my chest and drops to the floor in a metallic crash. A little spray peeps out of the nozzle. She shoves past me. "You're grounded. Two weeks. *Think*. Do it *right*."

———

Clare slips away from my life, as so many girls will do for the rest of my years in this town. At some point I see them in the halls at school and they're not in my universe anymore. I say hi and so do they and they keep moving.

But always there's a sense of loss. Girls baffle me. As one drifts away I struggle to understand why we weren't meant to stay best friends forever. I never comprehend. I have a lot of boys who are friends, and they make perfect sense to me. They shoot straight and always tell me, usually joking, what's what.

They tell me everything except the fact that they'd like to be more than friends. I don't pick up on this till it's too late.

Clare's departure brings me closer to Marie, my only friend until I discover Ruth, my best friend until her parents put her in the Baptist school in the eleventh grade. (For a second time, I prove too worldly.) Ruth doesn't like Marie. Marie lives in that nice house, indulges her mother's sugary bribes—and sews.

"You made this?" I ask. That something whole could emerge from hands, could be fashioned from . . . whole cloth . . . is astonishing. "How did you do it?"

She shows me her sewing machine in the corner of a special room, a whole extra room that she shares with her mother, who does embroidery and other crafts. There are two worktables and neatly stacked plastic drawers full of—well, the word turns out to be "notions."

Marie has really cool clothes. Little dresses, skirts, blazers.

"Wow," I say. "Cool," I say.

Junior high has been a social nightmare—I don't have any clothes. I tell my mother I want to sew like Marie.

My mother sees an opportunity.

She asks around town and finds that the local Singer shop offers lessons in the summer.

My mother makes me a deal.

"I'll buy you a sewing machine, and I'll pay for the lessons, and I'll pay for the fabric and everything else. But here's the thing—I'll buy you tops, but you have to make the bottoms."

I nod.

Mistake.

In the Singer store, I do learn the basics, but I become, during business hours, something of a lackey for Mrs. McCormack. If she's out back I stop cutting my pattern and all but wait on her customers. I bring her Cokes from the pharmacy next door and sandwiches from the deli up three blocks.

Where I come from, we have hot, humid summers. This is before Freons have conquered the nation, and the best Mrs. McCormack can do is open her door to the street. I'm in there twice a week for five weeks, until it's feeling like an extension of the sorts of expectations my mother has of me at home, that I'll step and fetch for her.

I do learn. Mrs. McCormack leans on me to cut threads at the end of a seam. Sew a seam, sew past the seam, pull out the thread, cut the thread right at the seam. Go back to the beginning of the seam *immediately!* and cut the thread of origin. "We don't like threads," Mrs. McCormack says over and over. "Threads are poisons." She's endlessly patient, not least because she's never really paying attention to me; she spends half our lesson staring out her window in the fullness of some boredom the likes of which I've never experienced—and when I make a mistake, she hushes my apologies. "Mistakes aren't a problem. Rip the seam. Do it again. See? Not a problem."

When I graduate from her tutelage, I have made a simple sheath, a sleeveless, A-line dress in kettlecloth, blue with small flowers, fitted closely to my curveless figure. She puts me on her hemming stand and pins the hem for me.

"You sure you want it that short?" she says.

I do learn. But, once home, I discover that my impulses toward perfection do not extend beyond the point at which the backache kicks in. My mother buys me, from Mrs. McCormack, a featherweight Singer, the kind with the sleek, arched arm, black with gold lettering, and nary bell nor whistle. It sews straight, and it sews in reverse. It sews straight and it zigzags. It sews seams and it sews base-stitch. That's all it does, if reliably. I set it up on the dining room table when I want to make something. I pin and cut my patterns in the basement, where the indoor-outdoor carpet has no nap; everywhere else in the house the pins attach the fabric to the rugs.

I'm getting really tall. I have to stoop to hear Marie when she speaks to me. And I certainly don't puff my chest out at home. I stoop to make the suddenly-short kitchen counters a bit closer to where I want them to be.

My father's gotten into the habit of walking up behind me and jamming a finger into my lumbar. It jolts me straight for a moment.

"Stand up straight," he says. "Put your shoulders back. Be proud you're tall."

This has little effect.

In the dining room I round my torso over the needle, foot on accelerator, moving as fast as I can. If I fuck up, who gives a shit, fuck it, keep moving, get this fucker done—and here's why: the pain starts just below my shoulder blades.

It's a high-pitched pain, a shrieker, and when it gets going nothing stops it. It edges up into the blades. Now it's screaming. It heads for the neck. I can't take it anymore. Just two more seams to go—*fuck! The zipper's crooked! Take it out and do it again! What? Are you shittin' me? Fuck it! Fix it by shortening the other side! I'm dyin' here!*

When my back gets horribly bad I lay flat on the floor, hitch my knees to my chest and squeeze desperately. When I drop my legs to the floor again, a secondary, lower-pitched ache settles into the lumbar. It's excruciating, but if I lie there long enough—about five minutes—the baritone pain will go away and the soprano pain eases.

My mother occasionally discovers me prostrate near my sewing machine.

"What the hell's wrong with you?" she says.

"My back."

"Well, get up. Clean this mess up. Set the table—Mr. Klavon is coming for supper."

I'm screwed. Marie has long since drifted out of my life, and just because I once wanted to be rich and cool like her, I'm enslaved to this stupid machine. And given my low tolerance for back pain, I'm limited to A-line skirts and pants with no waistbands, all in kettle-cloth or other cotton fabrics. When I'm a senior and find myself in dire need of a blazer, I take a bold stab at navy-blue linen—but double stitching, interfacing, buttonholes I have to cut by hand—it's a disaster. I wear it twice with the gray blouse my mother buys me, and throw it out.

I spend all of senior high not in jeans, like everyone else, but in faux-denim, back-dart, side-zipper bell bottom pants.

———

As it happens, I have a "late birthday," as school officials call it, and the Chester district wants me to wait till I turn five to enroll in kindergarten, but this would mean that I would shortly be six, and in kindergarten. My mother objects, gets the workbooks they use to teach kids to read and write, and—for lack of a better term—home-schools me through kindergarten. Quickly, I'm reading and writing at four. I start first grade at five, youngest kid in the class.

For the remainder of my education, I'm the youngest or nearly so.

I graduate at seventeen.

I leave home at seventeen.

———

I am being brought up well. My mother endeavors not to swear. "Shhhhhhhhhhhoot!" is what she yells when she jams her finger in a drawer. Upon receipt of any sort of gift I am required immediately to plop down at the kitchen table and write a thank-you note. I call my elders "Mrs." or "Mr." I am seen and not heard and am well liked in adult circles, which I enjoy, as I prefer adult conversations to any other kind. I know how to answer the telephone and know not to say my mother is not home, or worse, that she's taking a dump and can't be interrupted. "May I ask who's calling please? I'm sorry, she's indisposed at the moment—can I have her call you back?"

At table I do not reach. I say, "Pass the butter," and "Please," and "Thank you." I do not place my elbows on the table. I do not talk with my mouth full. I do not slump. I do not make a mess. I clean my plate. I say, "May I be excused?" I pick up after myself and take my plate to the sink. I do not expect to be waited on. I offer to help.

When I am twelve, and my brother is nine, my mother announces that she will no longer have supper with us.

"I can't stand your table manners," she says. "Your—noises. I just can't keep fighting with you about your manners. Eat like pigs if you want—I'm done with you. You're just too—*disgusting.*"

———

I am not a latchkey kid. I'm a German shepherd kid without the slightest need to lock the door.

My first chore on returning from school is to let the dog out. I open the backyard door and he dashes onto our small lot, liberated, lifting his leg on all four corners of the fence. The letting-him-out chore includes, in inclement weather, wiping his feet and legs down when he wants back in. Neither he nor I is thrilled at the prospect, but if he tracks mud on the rug, it's my ass, not his. Occasionally the letting-him-out chore includes a bonus chore: the cleaning-up-shit chore. If he shits on a rug because he really had to go, the pile will be downstairs by the door, where he meets me, his head skimming the floor. The house routine is to pick it up with paper towels, place it in a bag and then into the outside trash. Then I am to douse it with Pine Sol. That's what my mother smells when she comes home. "He went on the rug?" she says to me, angry already.

"Yeah."

"What—did you forget to let him out again?"

But there's a rather interesting alternative to the he-really-had-to-go scenario, and that's the he's-pissed-off scenario. Like us, dogs enjoy punishing whatever pissed them off. So he shits on purpose. Where does he shit on purpose? My room. Why my room? Well, the shag rug my mother installed there could be inviting, but really the problem is that my room is the only room in the house he's not allowed in. Why? I'm allergic to dogs. Thing is, the dog's not pissed at me. He's pissed at my mother—she left him alone too long, he's lonely, he didn't get fed—and he picks my room because he gets yelled at extra when he shits in there.

He consciously chooses to do the thing that will get him extra-yelled at.

Sometimes I really relate to him.

My second chore is to feed him. Half a can of stinky horse meat and an equal amount of dried food; add a little water and mash together. The beast has been nudging at me since he heard the electric can opener. I put the bowl down in a corner of the room and he drops his head in, pushes his snout up against the edge, slamming the bowl into the woodwork. Sunday, when next I clean the kitchen, I'll have to clean up his mess on the walls.

Other than at feeding time, the animal treats me rather haughtily.

He's the chosen one.

When my mother walks in from school, my brother and I are required to come downstairs and say hello. If we don't, we get screamed at and she's pissed right off the bat. Our primary task in life is to keep her not-pissed, so downstairs, gloomily, we trot, whereupon we feast unfed on the reunion of master and mutt. The dog goes apeshit-nuts, squeals, wags, grins, leaps up and leverages his paws on her shoulders, laps greedily at her face. She laughs, pets, scrunches up her mouth and lifts her chin to receive the kisses. "Hello," she says to him, "hello, how are you, hello, yes, I'm home, yes, hello, did you have a good day, OK, calm down, good boy, good boy, yes, he's a good boy—"

As her coat comes off and finds its way past fur and into closet, her eyes lift to two figures on the stairs. "Hi," she says.

"Hi," we say.

"How was school?"

"Good," we say.

"You get your grades yet?"

"No," we say.

"Any notes from your teachers?"

"No," we say.

She moves across the living room, dodging dog, and starts up the stairs.

We back away.

"You give me those grades the second you get them."

"OK," we say.

She's in the kitchen now. We back up the next flight of stairs toward our rooms. She picks up his empty dog bowl. "He get fed?" she says.

We're halfway up the stairs. "Yes," I call.

"You could've filled his water bowl."

She comes out, headed for her bedroom on the next landing. The dog follows, dropping to a spot near her door. "Get your homework done."

We slide back to our rooms.

———

For fun, my mother takes us to marching band practice, and at the age of nine I teach myself how to twirl a baton by watching the majorettes. From my four years of twirling I learn that discipline is easy when your desire to perfect something comes from you and you alone. I also find that I'm not the popular girl and never will be, but that merit will sometimes out. I'll never be in the clique but they vote me onto the squad anyway. I also discover in myself a dread of being watched—stage fright. I do ten doubles in a row in the backyard, but when I get nervous, I drop. All over the place. I spend a good deal of time in parades chasing a baton downhill, into the street's gutters. I determine that I have no social skills whatsoever— I know the other twirlers not in the least. On the fifty-yard line I scrunch my face and stick out my tongue while working through a horizontal. I also notice that fire doesn't always burn. And I find out that it's incredibly humiliating to have to call the head majorette of the junior high and tell her that your mother's making you quit the squad because you got a fucking D in algebra. Fucking algebra.

But what the hell. With my nervous condition I was never going to make the high school squad anyway.

"God," my mother says. "You and that tongue. You look like a squirrel. And that skirt of yours. It's only that short because you're so tall, but still—well, God—you look like a hooker."

———

When I'm in eighth grade my mother runs away from home without ever changing her address. For some time now she's been active in her teacher's union—"association," technically; it's an NEA chapter—and she's been appointed to the negotiating team. Association leaders like her; they press her to run for office. She gets elected president.

Our kitchen becomes a labor leader's mini-office. My telephone skills are taxed to maximum capacity, since she kicks up a roar whenever a message lacks some piece of information she needs. At times there are meetings in our living room—twenty of my past and future teachers waving good night to me as I deliver drinks in my pajamas and beat an exit. I sit on the steps upstairs and listen to them rant about how their school's being run.

This turn of events ramifies for my brother and myself in several ways.

The whole thing strikes me as entirely heroic.

And she's mostly gone.

She prosecutes major cooking offensives on Sunday, putting in the fridge stuff I can reheat, or fry, during the week. I add short-order cook to my list of chores.

And she's mostly gone.

Since she often doesn't get home till after we're in bed, I'm answering notes she's left for me with notes I've left for her. She and I rather enjoy this correspondence, which is often speckled with smiley faces and this thing called "love." As in, "Love, Mum." Or, "Love, Kass."

But she's mostly gone.

There are now a heap more things to get grounded for—I forget to mention a note from school saying my brother misbehaved again. The dog shits on the floor, I must have forgotten to let him out. I forget to leave a message that someone called. I fry two hamburgers and put the frying pan away dirty. I forget to call the person whose name I forgot about the thing I forgot and I don't reschedule my allergy shot—

"I know you're not *stupid*, so why do you *act* so stupid?" my mother shouts.

I'm trying to keep a good distance between us. She's in the kitchen where she has a beer and the light on, and I hover in the unlit dining room. "Get in here," she says. "I can't see you."

I take a nano-step forward.

"I need you to be *responsible*. Do you know what that means? Of course you know what that means. *Responsibility*. I can't do this by myself. Do you understand?"

She's mostly gone.

She's mostly gone.

She's mostly gone.

But also, the whole thing strikes me as entirely heroic.

———

One day we hear that Mrs. Patrick, next door, has died. My brother's no longer espoused to Trisha, the oldest daughter, who at fifteen suddenly exhibits her mother's exhausted, dejected air.

Mrs. Patrick was sick for a long time, we hear.

The thumps and hollerings continue, only now it's Trisha's voice we hear in protest.

––––

From fifth grade on my life, when it's not about twirling, is all about singing. My mother sings. My grandmother used to sing. We're all altos, although we never sing together. My mother has a two-octave range and good tonal qualities—none of the roundness required by classical performance, but pleasant tones. My voice is similar to hers, and we sing rounds in the car sometimes—but I have asthma. Most people think of asthma as being about inhalation ("Can't breathe!") but it's actually a disease of exhalation. Frequently I lack the force to thrum vocal cords, those chirpless organs, unless I suck on some albuterol first, but I don't learn about this drug till much later.

My mother and I work with the same voice teacher—an eccentrically brilliant man, too neurotic for New York so he teaches in our public high school—who can tell you far more than you want to know about any human cavity above the waist. And about this crazy little thing called a diaphragm.

But: that stage fright. Solos are impossible. My throat, which needs must be open (I practice yawning without opening my mouth), crushes shut.

At her concerts, my mother shakes and quivers but makes it through her solos fine. Consequently our voice teacher thinks me a victim of some freak congenital disease. Frequently he calls on me in class, as he calls on others: "Miss Fleisher!"

Gullet already jammed, I stand.

"Please read measures seventeen to twenty one."

I open my mouth, knowing that what will emerge will be a breathy horror. I begin measure seventeen, stumble through eighteen. I'm on key but there is no quality. I begin nineteen—

"Thank you!" he says, cutting me off. "That will do!"

His nostrils, which he flares for resonance, flap nearly to his ears.

It's the thing I most want that I most dramatically fail at. My singing career stops at college, because I can't audition solo.

Nonetheless, what I learn from music, besides practice practice practice, and how to pick out your part on a guitar, is the thrill of harmony with another human voice. The capacity for setting aside one-ness in the interest of a G minor. The transcendent experience of singing for hours and not knowing where the clock is. The aftershock of ambient resonance when, together, you cease your breaths.

———

"I never wanted kids," my mother says.

I try to appear sympathetic.

It's 9:30 at night, perfect time to ask for a prom dress. She's on her second beer. "I wanted to be a field biologist, but women weren't allowed to be field biologists, so I went to a teaching school, and I did teach biology for a while but that didn't work out, and I ended up having to use my English minor to teach English. Ridiculous. Now I'm stuck with this daaaaaaaaaaarn job."

She would like teaching better, she says, if a cadre of women didn't control the course assignments. "They stick me with the non-academic kids over and over and tell me it's because I'm such a good disciplinarian. Ridiculous. They horde the honors kids like you, keep you all to themselves. They tell me they have a stronger résumé than I do, that they took extra college courses or some shhhhh—

"I'm tired of talking—I need some quiet. You go upstairs now."

My mother is known for picking up those metal, institutional trashcans and walking up to a student sleeping at his desk during class. She drops the trash can right next to his head—all but blows him out of his chair. The other students laugh until she whips that look—that look!—across the room. Titters snap off. The kid settles back in his chair, eyes dull, takes a good look at the linoleum. My mother returns to her desk and takes up where she left off, nudging the class with questions about *Bless the Beasts and the Children*.

"None of them have read it," she says. "What's the point? They spend their afternoons in vocational school. They don't care if they ever read anything. They don't give a shhhhhh—"

If she ever changed a life, if she ever saw that spark, if she ever felt the need that can burn from a student's eyes, if she ever came home from school thinking, "That kid—that kid—I helped that kid *get* somewhere"—

—if she ever felt that sort of investment, and its concomitant dividend, she never told me.

———

The best part of life for my brother and me are the chunks of summer we spend in the mountains of central Pennsylvania with my mother's people, staying in her parents' tiny trailer on Tuscarora Mountain and hanging out with aunts, uncles, cousins, neighbors—rednecks to the bone, most of them. There's booze here, cards, long walks, creeks, bugs, critters, ruthless teasing and competition, bare-minimum tolerance—and no books. Local newspaper. *Good Housekeeping*, as if that were a goal.

My mother's oldest brother lives in a small town near the Mason-Dixon line, the kind you drive through in rural PA where porches, the width of their narrow houses, sit one after another after another after another, and at dusk every one of them is full of porch-setters watching cars, watching each other, gabbing idly in leaden air. My uncle has five kids—two more are hardly noticed. So he's good for a week. His oldest daughter, my age and beautiful—I'm in love with her—sits with me in her room playing Elvis's "In the Ghetto" over and over and over.

My mother's younger sister has two kids in a bigger town, a college town, actually, although her family has nothing to do with that—one of those small, private colleges on which Pennsylvania prides itself. She's good for a week too. Her oldest son, my age—I'm in love with him—races go-karts. He gets me situated in front of him on this beast he built himself, and charges me up and down the alley behind his house.

My mother's younger brother has a trailer a mile from my grandparents.

I have tightly tuned mother-radar—I know what she's feeling before she does, and what she's feeling is uncomfortable. She's thrilled to dump her kids but she doesn't want to hang around. What she wants more than anything else is not to have come out of what she came out of. Her main goal in life is to be *not this*.

So, youngish, she marries a fellow teacher's-college guy from the hills and moves to the city—but not really, just 'burbs. They rarely actually *enter* the city. But they're out of the hills. They class-transition up a notch.

Her sibling's kids never come stay at our house, although her parents visit us occasionally, my grandfather putting in a sump pump or building a door to close off the basement. Projects. That's what they do together. Little else.

The night before she drops us with her family, she pulls up, parks, chats, helps with supper, chats. Then they all drink. Next day, she leaves money for groceries, and heads out. "Behave yourself. Listen to your grandparents."

With which, she's backing down the gravel, kicking down the dirt road—and letting the games begin.

———

I'm a junior and my mother wants me to start thinking about where to go to college. College is all about getting a job, so which college I go to will be based on my vocational imaginings. So, she says. What do you want to be? she asks me. Like most parents, she's been through a long series of wanna-bes. The first thing I get serious about is astrophysics. Astronauts are the coolest thing since Wonder Bread and I take a math aptitude test in 7th grade, score high, enroll in an accelerated math program, in classes with kids a year ahead of me. I get an A the first term, but D's after that. Watching some guy's ass jiggle while he grinds chalkdust into air is not my idea of learning. Things don't improve when he dims the lights and winds his torso around an overhead projector.

Then it's journalism. Woodstein changed the world. I join the student paper, quickly rise in the ranks, scoop the local paper on the teacher's strike (I have an inside source). The student rag is laid out and printed at the local paper; I meet a lot of the writers when I drop off copy and photos. They're friendly, probably too friendly, to precocious rugrats running down the aisles in their newsroom. I see their behavior—the kidding, the teasing, the ribbing. I also see that there's only one girl there, and I see what happens one day when she bombs a lead on a page-one story. The guys tear out clips and roll them into balls, hollering, Here's how a real man writes a lead! and lob them at her desk. She laughs and leans back in her chair. These people, I tell my friend on staff at the student paper—they're too fucking competitive. What's up with them? They're all out to get each other.

By the time my mother asks I'm up to law. I want to be a lawyer, I say. What? she says. I want to be a lawyer. What do you think lawyers do? They help people. That's what you think they do? Yeah. Who do you want to help? Poor people. What poor people? You know, black people in the ghetto. You've been in a ghetto? No. Then how do you know what sort of help they need? I'll figure it out. How will you make a living if all you're helping is poor people who won't be able to pay you? I'll figure it out. You're going to open a storefront practice in the ghetto and you don't know how you'll get paid? I want to be a lawyer and help people. What in god's name do you know about lawyers?

A good deal, actually, since our entire domestic situation has been arranged by them, and my mother often calls my father at night, when she thinks we're sleeping, and shouts either that she's got one and he'll be hearing from them, or that she's thinking about getting one. But helping her, my father, me, or my brother is not my interest. I'm determined to help *other* people.

I call my father. He asks. I answer. Oh, Jesus, he says. What? I say. You want to be a lawyer? What is the problem with you people and lawyers? Let me ask you—what's a hundred lawyers chained to the bottom of the ocean? Excuse me? It's a good start. *Excuse* me? Where do you want to go to school? I'm thinking about Temple. Oh, Jesus. *Now* what? No, he says. *What?* That's a *really* bad neighborhood. *What the hell does that mean?*

There's a long pause as my father considers my years-long tendency to get fresh with him in a heartbeat.

Those people, he says, don't live right, and I won't have you in that neighborhood. *Excuse me?* It's a bad neighborhood—you stay out of there. Did you just call them *those people*? You heard me. *Those people*? Christ, Dad. You're such a fucking *racist*. The answer is no—you won't be doing any schools in the city.

He'll be contributing $2,500 a year to the project—half. That gets him a big vote. I'll earn the other half working in the local tile factory, summers, rotating from job to job to cover for vacationing regulars. Yeah—back then you could make a semester's costs on a factory floor, especially with piecework. I date another summer kid there, Lehigh engineering student, scary-smart guy. Great motivation, isn't it? he says to me one day. What do you mean? I ask. This place. He waves his arm across the hot, silent factory, people perched everywhere with their faces in their lunch. They lift their eyes occasionally to squawk about the Phillies. Super Steve, Iron Mike, Tug Mac, Tim Mac, etc. Fucking Larry Bowa's batting less than .300, fucking Maddox too, Luzinski too the fucking pansy but Jesus, 100 RBIs, Christ! At least when Luzinski hits it fucking *counts*! There's no lunch whistle. Just an ingrained clock that says your thirty minutes is up. Time to fire up the forklifts. Dump a pallet of tile. People stand up to the roar as the monster assembly line lights up. Great motivation to stay in college! my boyfriend shouts, hurrying away. His gig is on the other side of the building. He's already late.

———

In eleventh grade, without ever considering it consciously, I take a lesson from my mother and run away from home without even changing my address. I become president of everything. I go to school early, for madrigal rehearsals. I stay late, for chorus practice, the student newspaper, and the student environmental action group. Today they would call me an "amazing girl," or "organization kid"—three-point-god-knows-what GPA, top ten percent of my class, School Leader.

The only thing missing is sports, and that's thanks only to my asthma. Oh, and I want to join the drama club, but rehearsals run later than the extracurricular bus, and my mother says, "Only if you can get a ride. I don't have time to chauffeur your ass all over town."

I'm not capable of asking for help of any sort, up to and including a ride home. I don't know how I get elected to so many posts—I'm convinced none of the kids like me. It's my teachers, the club advisors, who encourage me to run for things. I think they know I'm reliable beyond any human notion of reliability. I'm the perfectionist that ate Cincinnati.

And I sure could use some fucking positive feedback, which is maybe why I'm so keyed on doing all this stuff, and doing it right. But it doesn't hurt that I don't get home till 6:00 most days.

"God knows what your brother's up to till you get home," my mother says—but she doesn't stop me from (essentially) abandoning ship. I get home, put supper on, ride my brother's butt to get his homework done, yell at him because now it's his job to let the dog out and feed him. I clean house, start on my own homework, get on the phone and talk to other kids in the clubs, organize. Machinate this and that. Write articles for the paper, find someone to put up posters for the CROP Walk for Hunger, work the scrap-paper machine, proof the program for our next concert.

People tell me I'm a born organizer, but they don't know that I simply spent junior high watching my mother do it.

———

Mine is the first generation of girls to grow up with Title IX in our pockets.

I really want to be a boy. Really truly. I declare it as loudly as I declare my atheism at fourteen. With my father, I'm Number One son.

Ultimately, I do throw like a boy, but that's the best I can do. Menstruation persists. I don't do competition well. That nervous condition.

My mother throws a ball (baseball, mainly), my brother drops it, she gets pissed. "I threw that right to you!" she says. "That was right in your glove—what's wrong with you?"

Five most dreaded words to emerge from my mother's mouth on a Sunday afternoon: "Wanna throw the ball around?" Gutscrunch immediately. Strive, strive. Put the ball in the glove. Wind up and throw with your stomach—that's what my brain is being told. She's gonna yell, she's gonna blow, it's just a matter of time—

"What the hell," she says, neglecting her ban on swearing. "What the hell was that. You call that throwing a baseball?"

Volleyball. She likes volleyball. "Men always hog the territory," she says. "The ball's coming right at you and they shove you away." It's hard for three of us to pop a ball back and forth over a net—the only logical configuration is us against her. "Come on, keep it up, keep it going. Call it. You've got to call it. Use your fingertips. What are you doing? I hit that ball right at you! Did you *duck* that *ball*? Don't duck the ball—what is *that*?"

Competitive sports are about responsibility. If the ball comes at you, you owe it to your team to fucking get it.

Both of my parents were jocks, my mother a swimmer and my father a basketball player. This could have been what they bonded over. But with ball in hand, my father is different with kids. My father corrects errors of approach. His is a pedagogy of adjustment. He throws the ball and then says, "Try lifting your glove so it's there when you need it." If my brother drops a ball, he says, "Pick it up. Throw it to your sister. Good."

He keeps me well stocked in sporting goods. One year I ask for a football. That I'm a girl causes not a hiccup. A football I get. I wind up my shoulder and let one loose. "It's not a baseball," he says, chasing the tumbling oval along the parking lot of the bar where he hangs out. It's next door to the crappy apartment he lives in for thirteen years. "Line up your fingertips along the seam." In ten minutes I'm throwing perfect spirals, but it's taking all my shoulder to do it. "Let me see," he says, walking over to me. He takes my hand and places it on the ball. "Your hands are too small. The velocity's coming out of your shoulder because you can't get your hands around the ball."

He takes it upstairs to his apartment and soon comes back with it, slightly deflated.

I play touch football down the street with the neighbor kids for years, with that slightly deflated football. No one notices a thing.

But I'm way better at throwing than catching. *Responsibility! Everyone will get mad at me if I miss!* I frequently do miss. Stage fright. In those three seconds of hang time, the spotlight's on me. *I'm going to miss it!*

Because of asthma, it never becomes an issue. Join the volleyball team and *run laps? Are you high?* One lap and I'm heaving, bronchi pinched, exhalation a full-body workout. Later I learn that albuterol can be used *before* the bronchi get the chance to close, and sometimes I wonder—if I'd been a 5'11", trim, fairly athletic *boy,* would my doctor have suggested that earlier? Would my mother have pressed to improve my medical options?

What I learn post-Title IX: Coaches are cool. I get along with my male teachers way better than my female teachers.

———

Three o'clock. Weekday. On the school bus. Down Main Street, down Cannon Avenue, past the factory, past the Little League parks.

Bus takes a left turn into our development.

Butterflies launch just shy of esophagus. Colon grabs.

This as soon as we hang that Louie.

Five o'clock. Sunday. My father's car. It's his weekend with us, he drives us home. Down Main Street, down Cannon Avenue, past the factory, past the Little League parks.

Takes a left turn into our development.

Butterflies launch just shy of esophagus. Colon grips and twists.

Soon as we hang that Louie.

Eight o'clock. Saturday. My first husband's car. We've been away on vacation for two weeks, are driving home. I'm twenty-seven. Down High Street, down West Avenue, past the pizza place, past the library.

Take a right turn onto our street.

Butterflies dance just shy of esophagus. Colon twists and jerks.

Soon as we make that turn.

At age five, my brother develops a stutter.

By the time I'm fifteen I'm seeing three specialists. I have eczema on my hands, treated by a dermatologist who prescribes a cream, places my fingers under a blue light, and leaps upon zits, which he will stop to pop in quick succession.

"Don't try this at home," he says.

At home, my mother insists that I wash the dishes in the hottest water I can get out of the faucet. I wear rubber gloves. Many times she walks into the kitchen as I work, sticks her finger into the water, and snaps, "I said hot water!" My hands, in gloves and heat, sweat, which burns the eczema. After supper, my hands blaze red.

I hear her on the phone to my father, who, in the much-regaled divorce settlement, makes the minimum child support payment but saves for our college education and pays my medical bills. "How should I know why—she's got some kind of allergic reaction to rubber gloves I think. It doesn't matter. A bill's a bill."

I have some kind of neck problem, treated by an orthopedic surgeon who insists that nothing structural is wrong, welcoming our appointments but shrugging at my mother afterwards. Still, I can't turn my head to the left. I sleep at night with a heating pad on my pillow. My jaws click open and shut, thudding with each bite, and a girl in the cafeteria shoots me an unflattering look one day. "Ew," she says. "I can hear all your chews!" My junior year in high school my jaw freezes open and I can't bite into a cheeseburger until summer.

"He said 'TMJ,'" my mother says into the phone. "*You* ask him what it is."

And of course there is my allergist. We do the requisite shots for years, my mother driving me every Friday after school to be poked by his nurse, and I'm damn glad to see her, too, because sometimes she's busy with a line of kids and *he* comes in, and that motherfucker couldn't give a decent shot if his practice depended on it, which it doesn't in high-pollen, high-mold, southeastern PA. Occasionally he puts me through a round of back scratching—allergy tests.

"Wow," his nurse says, "look at that. You're really allergic to cats. Huh," she continues, "you're allergic to dogs but not as bad."

"I don't know why he had to do the test again," my mother says into the phone. "Take it up with him."

When my father picks us up for a weekend, I am tasked with handing him our medical bills. Since my brother, like her, is never sick, they're all mine. I hand them over and absorb his wince.

———

In seventh grade my spine stretches for sky and I'm suddenly taller than god. I hover over my teachers, over the kids at the bus stop, over my brother. My father's tall—most-valuable-high-school-hoop-player tall. My mother's average, a squirt next to us.

I'm taller than she is now.

"Kass!"

My belly snatches south. My brother and I are sitting on the floor watching television, enjoying our permitted one hour per day. As he often does, the dog snores at his post in front of the door.

She stomps across the dining room to the landing above us, shaking the floor as she goes.

The dog lifts his head.

"Kass!"

"What?" I say. I'm developing a temper. We only get one hour, for godsake.

"Don't speak to me in that tone!"

I rephrase. "What?" I ask.

"Which one of you drank my Fresca?"

"What?"

"Don't play games with me. Which *one* of you drank my *Fresca*?"

"What are you talking about?"

She's lickety-split down the six steps to the living room, heels digging worn rug. The dog gets up and goes downstairs. She grabs us each by the collar and yanks. My brother ejects easily—me, I'm stuck. All she succeeds in doing to me is cutting my collar into my neck.

She lets go.

I roll around on my hips to face her. Hanging onto my brother's collar, she lowers her head toward mine. "I'm asking you for the last time. Which one of you drank my Fresca?"

I lean back onto my hands. "I have no idea."

She kicks her toes into my legs, jerking my brother along with each kick. I pull my legs out of the way and she kicks along after me, my brother tugged behind, until she finally has me cornered between the TV stand and the chair next to it. I pull my legs to my chest and now she's getting only shinbone, the chair bumping along until it hits wall.

She moves in for one last boot and then backs off and lets go of my brother.

"Stand up when I talk to you," she says to me.

I heave myself off the rug.

I'm five inches taller, easily. I drop grenades down into her stupid, stupid eyes.

She takes a step back. She looks at my brother.

"It was you, wasn't it?" she says.

"Was not!" my brother says.

"It's always you. How many times do I have to tell you, there's *your* food and *my* food, and you eat *yours*, and I eat *mine*." She raises her hand to swat my brother's butt.

"Look!" I bark.

"What?" she says.

"Nobody—drank—your fucking—Fresca. Nobody—fucking—touched it."

"Go to your room!" she screams.

"With pleasure!" I yell. I stomp across the room and up the stairs.

"You too!" she hollers at my brother, who races up behind me.

———

My mother at school. "At school" is synonymous with "at work," or "at the office," which is strange—my mother goes where I do during the day. "How was school today?" I ask her on occasion, just as she asks me. This makes me her coworker, her my fellow student—which is wrong—so what is the right relation?

My mother in the halls: giant grin on her face. To look at her as she passes from teacher's lounge to classroom, or from classroom to office—she appears thrilled by the possibility of encountering fellow creatures. Very pretty, she is. Polyester pantsuit, moderate heels, auburn hair flipped like Mary Tyler Moore, whom she resembles (but more strikingly, she resembles Susan Hayward, none of whose films I've ever been able to sit through without a gutache)—blue eye shadow, mascara, no lipstick—her gait is peppy as she negotiates the flow of kids ambling off to a class they don't want to take in a factory town where most of them have a job on the side so they can pay for the Chevelles, Firebirds, and Shelbys that clog the school parking lot. She hits the passing lane with verve, purpose in her stride.

I never fail to see her first, even though I'm taller than anyone in the river of kids on my side of the hall. I'm looking for her; she's not looking for me. My throat tightens. I'm usually in the passing lane myself, so we're about to bump elbows.

"Hi," I say, smiling as broadly as she is.

She's jolted every time. "Oh my God!" she says, hand flying to her neck. "Hi!" I'm not where I belong, I'm in the wrong space, I'm in *her* space—she looks even more delighted than she did when she was simply walking with that anticipatory look on her face. "See you later," I say. "Yeah," she says excitedly. "Later!"

———

I don't begrudge her the spankings, even though they aren't infrequent, and I don't like her methods: "Get upstairs and get my hairbrush!"—bare behinds—forty lashes, or it feels like it anyhow. I do resent the ones that feel undeserved. But even then, spankings possess a ritual aspect that lends a mutually respectful air to our relative roles. Her parent, me child. Whether or not I actually fucked up, her anger is controlled.

I don't begrudge her the spankings.

———

From the time my mother becomes a member of the negotiating team, she suddenly has eyes everywhere. From her union activities, she knows every teacher we have.

In seventh grade, my first boyfriend's name is Glenn. I know next to nothing about him—I don't think we so much as talk. It is necessary that I have a boyfriend—it is not necessary that I actually like him. He wears denim jackets and dirty boots and jeans and sneaks outside to smoke between classes, and that's all I need to find him wildly interesting, whether he possesses conversational skills or no. And apparently he does not. For the seventh grade dance, I sew a skirt so short and tight that, surely, I'm shooting beaver to all four winds. Glenn and I slow-dance, me some distance taller, and that's all. When fast songs come on we wander outside, make out in the building's shadows. He gives me a friendship ring that turns my finger black. When a slow song comes on we go back to the dance floor.

"So," my mother says, "I'm told you've been making out in the halls with some boy."

I stare at the green vinyl kitchen tablecloth. I have an obsessive habit of braiding the fringe, with the result that the tablecloth within reach of my usual seat at table is entirely braided. When necessary I unbraid a strand and rebraid it.

"This isn't the kind of behavior I want from you," she says.

She speaks firmly but mildly.

"I don't like it. Kids do it all the time. It's disgusting that every time we change classes we're confronted with these people slobbering all over one another."

I fiddle with the fringe.

"I know it's supposed to be cool to do that, but it's disgusting. Don't do it."

I unbraid a strand.

"So who is this boy, anyway?"

I never tell my mother anything about my personal life, my crushes, my friendships, my sex life when I have one, my desires, my passions, my loves.

Nothing. Ever. Nada. Zilch.

"God, you're so private," my mother bursts out one day when she's on a fishing expedition about a possible tenth-grade boyfriend. This one wants to be a pilot, wants to join the Air Force. Flying enthralls me, liberation from gravity, defiant possibilities of machinery; he's trying to recruit me into the Civil Air Patrol's wing for kids. She suspects the can-I-join-the-CAP query is about a boy but can't pin me down. "God," she says, exasperated. "You're so *secretive*. Why are you *like* that? What's going on in that *head* of yours?"

"So what's this boy's name?" my mother says.

"Glenn."

"Got a last name?"

The braids go together without my looking at them anymore.

"Who is he?"

"Just a guy," I say.

Just this once, and only this once, it's the truth.

"Just a guy," my mother says, as if repeating it will provide further illumination.

I can braid these strands in my sleep. In fact, I often do.

———

Because my mother now knows all and sees all, I take great pains to be as perfect as possible. "You realize," my mother says, "that because of my position with the association, if you get caught with drugs, it'll be on the front page of the newspaper."

I'm perfection itself. I'm the walking illustration of perfection. I'm the perfection of perfection.

My brother, on the other hand, has a different reaction. "Fuck her," he says to me as I beg him, beg him, *beg him* to behave himself.

"I'm living my life. The fucking newspaper is her fucking problem."

———

My mother hates it when I get sick. The depth of the inconvenience to her is unfathomable. She has the bedside manner of Cinderella's stepmother.

"Get the thermometer," she says, on hearing me call down the stairs to say I have a cold. "Take your temperature." I hear a long string of whispered cuss-words. "What is it," she calls upstairs with zero compassion.

"Hundred and one point two," I wheeze.

She mounts the stairs, pounding each one with the soles of her low-heeled shoes.

The dog misinterprets the situation and heads downstairs.

"You coughing?"

Only all night, and don't know how she could've missed it, but yes.

"Runny nose? What? Tell me what's happening."

I long to be no bother. *Long. To be no. Bother.*

"Stay in bed. I'll call you."

"Sorry," I say.

She doesn't respond.

My brother whispers his own string of cuss-words. "I never get to stay home," he says as she bellows his name from below.

"Do not," she hollers, "miss that bus, boy. My day is already bad."

As she leaves she lobs one last salvo up the steps. "Bed!" she says. "Read! No TV!"

As soon as they're gone, I scoot downstairs with a blanket and turn it on. The UHF stations air old reruns all day, giving my sick days an air of nostalgia for good old times never experienced—Mayberry, New Rochelle, wherever it is that Lucy and Ricky live. At 1:00, Channel 48 plays old movies with Jimmy Stewart, Bette Davis, Gary Cooper, Katherine Hepburn.

Her calls are predictable, coming between her classes. She calls the first time at 8:57.

I know how many rings it takes to get from my room to the phone in the kitchen. That's how many I let ring.

"I got a doctor's appointment at four o'clock," she says. "Are you in bed?"

"Yeah," I say.

"Stay in bed. I'll be home at lunchtime with Robitussin."

At 11:45, so the TV has time to cool off, I abandon Jim West and his friend Artie and head up to bed. She walks in at 12:15, drops her coat around surprised dog noise and heads up the stairs. "Here," she says. She pours sticky red syrup into a spoon and aims the spoon for my head as I sit up in bed. My lip bumps the edge of the spoon and a drop falls on my nightgown. "Christ almighty," she says, "don't *spill* it." She pounds downstairs and comes up from the bathroom with a wet washcloth. "Clean yourself up," she says. "I'll pick you up at three forty-five sharp," she says. "Be dressed and ready to go."

When my brother gets home from school he finds me in front of the TV, well into whatever's happening with Bob Newhart's wacky friends.

"Cheater," he says.

Once, my brother and I overlap for about three days on the same case of the measles.

Now *that*, as they say—*that* was *a good time.*

———

If I heard it once, I heard it a million times: "I've never asked him for an increase in child support," my mother lectures, "not once, not ever, and I took the lowest support level the court offered on the condition that he pay your medical bills—you get your asthma from *his* mother, after all, not mine—and save money for your education. I had to fight for my education and I didn't want you to have to fight for yours. So I've done without—but you'll get an education."

I leave home, after a long slow wait, at the end of a senior-year summer during which I work two jobs, twelve hours a day. I'm seventeen, but my adult coworkers in the filing office of the county's unemployment tax office take me to lunch, order me tuna-melts, and teach me to drink. Determined for years to stay off the front page, I'm neither a drinker nor a pothead—another source of social alienation—but my parents have demonstrated that all adults do it. Drink, that is. And I'm transitioning into adult-drink-world, so—here's how!

Green in the office at two in the afternoon, I tell a coworker that I think I'm going to puke. She gives me Pepto-Bismol, with the result that I puke pink.

I'm sober, if sick, by the time I grab a sandwich downtown and hit my evening job. I'm phoning homes on behalf of the Fraternal Order of Police. I'm telling people that the FOP is bringing a circus to town, and asking them to pay six dollars to sponsor a seat for a retarded kid. I have a cousin who's retarded—a word I can barely articulate orally—and all of this strikes me as truly fucked up, but it's before the days of relentless telephone solicitation, and I actually get into long, chummy chats with strangers.

I'm paid in cash. My mother insisted I get my first summer job when I turned fourteen, cleaning other people's houses. Since then, she has taken my checks, given me a five-spot, and slapped the rest in the bank "for college." She knows how much I make per hour with the FOP—but she doesn't know about the bonuses.

I make a lot of bonuses.

All of which go straight to the guy on Main with the little record shop. Illegally, he sells me his sample records ("Not for sale!") for two bucks a pop. "You must have a good collection," he says to me. But records have never been about collecting for me—I don't grasp this notion at all. Records are forty-five minutes of elsewhere, someone else's elsewhere, someone else's grasp of my world, someone else's perfect harmony. I'm told my taste is eclectic, but my taste is all about who's singing well—specifically, who's using technique, so that when I sing along with them (it's impossible for me not to sing along), I'm learning to sing well too. Since I'm an alto, high tenors are square in the middle of my range, and in 1976 and 1977, all I care about are the Eagles, Queen, and—well, anything Simon or Garfunkel. Foreigner, Kansas, Heart—I'd give my right tit to be Ann Wilson—Fleetwood Mac, and—well, anything Mamas or Papas—then The Voices: John Denver, Barry Manilow—go ahead, laugh, but those fuckers could sing—

It never occurs to me to buy records by women and people of color, but my ear hangs waiting, waiting on the Philly radio stations to play dance music—just about anything Motown—

—Philadelphia Atlantic—

—and Carly, Carol, Joan, Judy—

—Linda—

Lyrics are muscle memory. Play me one bar of a vocal arrangement and I can tell you precisely where in the song you are. And lyrics instruct. In my ligaments, learnings. "Where did all the blue skies go?" "Does anybody really know what time it is?" "War—huh—what is it good for?" "How can a loser ever win?"

Writer of my life story—even though my story, come to find, is not hers: Janis Ian.

Streisand. Streisand, a canyon's cavity on two legs. My mother and I have long discussions about whether she could get a nose job and still maintain that lift.

"Have a drink, have a drive—go out and see what you can find."

I can do step harmony in my sleep. I *do* do step harmony in my sleep. Think about it—one voice mediates, maintains responsibility for the gaps, the fissures between the melody, the descant, and dissonance. You, over there—and you, over there: stay there! Boundaries inviolable. Failure to resolve: horror.

2.

The second teacher I ever met was my mother's second husband. He's an English teacher too, not to mention coach of girls' tennis, but in a different school district. For me he unfurls a string of epithets.

Prickfuckheadcocksuckerdouchebagasswipeshitheadthumb-dickdickheaddick.

Amen.

On the plus side, we move to the country, and I do third and fourth grades in a remote area between the two districts, living on an acre lot with trees, grass, forest. My mother's Chester-born security force, who's grown up to be an elegant and quite rare white shepherd—with papers—comes along and runs happily in the country, no more close-cropped row-home neighbors at which to howl. Dickhead and my mother decide to make extra money breeding him, so they buy a dark, sleek bitch, so perfect she's doomed to hip dysplasia, and for two years my brother and I hang around at dog shows in puppy heaven. It's clear we're really country kids. We like roaming the outdoors in any dry weather, on room-sized boulders where we play house, torture daddy-long-legs, slam snowballs.

We like roaming in any dry weather anywhere those two aren't going to be. The fights start promptly, are epic, go on for days. Silent treatment seems to be the primary conflict strategy. Mute tension is broken only by the sound of ice cubes in a glass.

His poison is whiskey.

The fights are usually over money. My mother, who could squeeze a dime from a nickel, sits at the dinner table over a plate of her own perfect meatloaf and announces that she can't afford to buy me socks. Since my personal expenses are frequently the source of arguments between my biological parents—especially my medical bills—this conversation is sorely disruptive to my digestion. Thus begins my first-ever eating disorder.

"May I be excused?

"You haven't eaten your supper."

"I'm not hungry."

"You'll clean your plate."

With that, the epic battle ceases to be my socks and becomes my plate. Cocksucker gazes across the table at me with a smirk across his face. I've become a bigger ass than he is—I deflect, he wins.

Battles royale erupt about my appetite. I hate peas—she stands over me for three hours until I eat every last frozen one of the bastards. Prick's in the living room tinkling his glass, happy.

I hate mushroom soup—she abandons me at table and returns to find that I have regurgitated into the bowl. I sit there till I've eaten every last revolting drop of bile in the bowl. Shithead rattles his glass.

But my bedtime is 8:00, so I can't protect her beyond that hour, which is when the real drinking goes on. They yell, he slaps her around, I hear thumps—I'm sure she hits him back. I know from personal experience that she's a scrappy fighter. She gets her licks in, I'm sure. I'm sure Douchebag has some bruised shins.

We get home from school some time before either of them, and are baby-sat by the woman next door, Mrs. Heller, with her six kids in tow, all of whom are addicted to *General Hospital*. When we see a car in the drive, we are to return.

Sometimes Prick gets home first.

We drag our asses down the road, look back over our shoulders, don't want to go. We walk in. He's at the table—or maybe the puppies need fed—or maybe he's just sitting on his ass. We say hi, he grunts, nothing beyond that gets said. I stop in the kitchen for an apple—he sits. I make my way to my room.

Hatred hangs.

Towards the end, when none of the puppies are staying white like their sire and money's extra-tight and booze flows extra-hard, Asswipe knocks her around but good. Furthermore, Thumbdick finds himself in *my* room late at night, sticking his greasy, shithead, douchebag fingers into my pint-sized orifice. What a fucking dick.

And no, I never told my mother about it.

One night he socks her bad, and it ends. I don't know how, but I can tell it's the end from my room down the hall. My mother sobs, screams, hurls something that shatters. The tall shepherd growls in his killer-warning tone. I stand in my dark bedroom. There's a moon, shadow of bare trees banging in wind. Thump, shriek. Every time I've left my room I've been ordered to return, but this time my mother is dying. This is different—I can hear her crying—I should leave the room and save her—but how will I save her—all these animals so much bigger than me—bigger—my mother is dying.

I walk into the hall, not sure which to fear more: my mother's scolding for being out of bed, or my mother's demise. I fear both equally.

Thump, shriek.

When I appear in the bright-blinding living room, as my pupils jam shut to close out the light, Dick looks at me in shock. I'm the blackened cinder in his reddening retina. He bellows something, picks up his coat, leaves.

My mother clutches her ribs. We sit on the couch and listen to the sound of the car backing out of the drive and down the road in front of our lot.

The dog has followed him to the door, stays there, erect, paws up on the window. When the car sound is gone he drops to the floor, lies down, stations himself there.

That's a good dog.

My mother and I sit and watch Johnny Carson. She's got two ribs broken.

"You should go to a doctor," I say.

"Can't," she says, every breath a chore.

"Why not? They hurt you."

"If I go to a doctor they'll have to know how I broke them. If I tell them he did it, they might arrest him."

Sounds like a good idea to me, I don't say.

We move out of the country a month later, into the row-home development in the town where my mother teaches. She keeps only one of the dogs—her majestic, white Lancelot.

Asshole's first wife calls my mother when she hears of the breakup. She tells my mother that the prick pulled a knife on her. Corroborating information is perhaps better late than never, but *late*. Shortly, my mother sees an engagement announcement in the paper, a pretty blonde—his next victim. My mother tells me she's thinking of contacting the woman, warning her.

She decides against.

This is when I have my first experience with shunning.

I ask my mother something about the dick, the douchebag, something irritated, and she snaps at me.

"Don't talk to me about him."

"What do you mean?"

"I just want to forget all about him."

Within a week or so, I forget the new rule, and mention something else, something doubtless aggravated.

"I told you already, don't ask me about him, or mention his name. I never want to hear about him again. Now, I told you that already."

"I don't understand."

"Yes you do. It's over. Don't bring him up again, ever, and I mean it."

With regard to his nocturnal thumb in my aperture, I suffer no ill effects. All of the conditions for post-abuse recovery are firmly in place. The entire family agrees the shithead was a cocksucker. I'm free to hate the creep. He's been removed from my environment. That he beat my mother only makes it more clear that he's evil—I suffer no confusion about whether his nocturnal tours are my fault—I don't even repress the memory—since the perpetrator is so depraved his name may not be spoken ever again.

P-R-I-C-K.

For whatever reason, though, my mother doesn't change her name back, so in this way, Asswipe's name is spoken every day.

This has the effect of giving me a tidbit of anonymity when I finally move up to my mother's high school. Kids don't know she's my mother—thus I'm told repeatedly at lunch tables what a bitch she is. But generally my teachers find out through parent-teacher exchanges.

One day my gym teacher approaches me. She coaches the girls' tennis team, and tells me that Prick's had trouble on the job—he got fired from coaching for patting his players' asses and making inappropriate comments. Now he's had a heart attack and has had to take a leave. She thinks my mother should know but she can tell it's a touchy subject.

My teacher asks me to tell her.

Good Christ.

I agonize all day long, get home around suppertime and blurt it out to her.

She's furious.

"I told you never to mention him to me again!"

"I'm sorry, I just thought—"

"Don't think! I don't want him in my head! God, I was having a halfway-decent day and you have to come home with *this* bullshit, when I've told you and told you—go to your room! Christ! I want him OUT OF MY HEAD!"

———

You can always tell a geeknerdthroat by whether they went to their senior prom, and I didn't. No junior prom either, although as a junior I get asked to someone else's senior prom. He's gorgeous, another social alien, but not of an intellectual or artistic bent. He's been tossed off our lousy football team—and he has a crush on my mother.

My mother insists on meeting all of my "boyfriends." As if we're talking about a long string.

"Wow, your mom is *cool,*" he breathes as he walks me to his muscle car.

Now that I've learned to keep my mouth shut, anyone who meets my mother says that. Occasionally we're confused for sisters. Nothing cheers her more than hearing this. She's a flirt, actually. Around anyone but family, her dark eyes sparkle, her auburn hair swings, always a bright smile and quick laugh on the ready. She asks people about themselves—nods, beams.

I wait for her second beer before I go downstairs and lurk in the shadows of the dining room. I tell her Rick asked me to his prom.

"Can I get a prom dress?"

"I'll buy you fabric for it," she says.

Curses!

So I go as a junior to the senior prom (bit of a social promotion!) wearing the ugliest prom dress in the history of the world. Kettlecloth won't do, of course, but I can't work with anything really fine—the polyester fabric I choose, with minimal drape, is a lime green. I select the simplest pattern I can find, a day-dress pattern with the option for lengthening to the floor. V-neck; cap sleeves; and, because I'm convinced I'm fat, empire waist.

To fancy it up a bit I select a kelly-green synthetic lace border to sew along the neckline.

My usual 10:00 P.M. curfew is lifted, provided I explain where we're going to be. Itinerary: dinner on the Main Line, drive back to the prom, after-party at the home of a football player my mother's had in class. She doesn't like the kid but she recalls his mother from parent-teacher conferences and feels OK about it.

Rick and I spend nearly all the prom in the backseat of his Camaro, which I kind of mind—I want to experience a prom, and after-parties with the jock crowd must be cool!—but not really. I don't really want to be seen in public in this fucking dress.

And being nowhere I'm supposed to be, and walking in at four in the morning—now *that's* cool.

———

The clock in my room says 10:16. I hear the front door open, close, hear the dog going quietly nuts, hear her make her pet noises, hear her start up the stairs to the living room and kitchen, a large mass of dog bouncing around her. I hear her go to the kitchen, hear some rustling.

"Jesus Christ," I hear her mutter.

My belly bores holes through my lungs.

She walks into her bedroom, dog lapping behind. Her shoes hit the walls with a crack.

My eyes gape.

Stockinged feet thump with purpose on the stairs. Light snaps on, covers strip back, arm jerks.

"Get up."

I'm all but out of bed when she gets there. Quickly she's in my brother's room. "Get up." She's got him by the arm, drags his half-unconscious body down the steps. I follow behind, compelled by her threatening glare in the hallway.

We're dropped in the kitchen. My brother blinks his eyes furiously. She grabs a bag of half-eaten Oreos.

"Who ate the Oreos?"

The dog exits.

I stare at her. She yanks my brother's unresponsive arm. "Who?" she demands. "Who ate the Oreos?"

I stare at Captain Queeg with a mutinous eye.

Her hand is across my face before I can blink.

"We had some after supper," I say, stepping back.

"How many?"

"Four, like always."

We're allowed four each after supper every night.

Sometimes we sneak extra.

"How many did you have?"

"Four." In this instance I'm pretty sure I'm right.

She jerks my brother's arm. "Did you have extra?"

"Extra what?" my brother says.

She tosses him across the galley kitchen, where he crashes against cupboards.

"Get over here," she says to me.

Micro-step forward.

"Do you see these?" She picks up the bag of Oreos. "I counted them. I know how many were in there when I left. There are twelve missing. You're saying you had eight. Where did the other four go?"

I stare at her.

I may be out of range for another slap, but with one step she lands a lightning kick to my shin.

"Liars!" she says. "If there's one thing I can't stand it's lies!"

"Get up!" she yells at my brother. He gets to his feet. "Upstairs!"

she hollers. I beat a hasty exit ahead of both of them. My brother rapidly finds my heels—he's awake now. "My room!" she bellows.

My heart sinks. *Her room*? Her room is the *worst place in the house* to be in trouble.

She shoves past us as the dog gets down from the bed and heads heavy-hung down the steps. She crashes into her walk-in closet.

"Who touched these?"

She returns with an Al Stewart record and a new model ship, the destroyer-class USS Iowa, for my brother's expanding collection.

OH, FUCK.

CHRISTMAS.

"Who touched these?"

I look at my brother.

"I didn't get near 'em!" my brother howls.

"Bullshit!" my mother snaps.

"Did not!"

My mother trains her coal-eyes on me. "Did you? Were you in here?"

I'm terrified of my mother's room. Aside from dusting it, which I do as quickly as possible, as if I'm in the warden's office—a place in which there'd be dire consequences if I were found—

"Were you?"

"Just to vacuum."

"Vacuum?" She drops the record on the bed and lunges quick enough to get a chunk of hair. "Vacuum, or sneak through what was supposed to be a surprise?"

"Vacuum," I say.

On orders, I roll the vacuum cleaner across the shag carpet in the closet, taking pains to ignore the shoe boxes stacked on the top shelf, or the polyester pantsuits lining the rack.

My brother takes the prohibition as more of a challenge. "You know she's got a gun up there?" I follow him up and peek at it with two kinds of terror churning my gorge. "Stay out of here!" I snap.

"I told you kids and told you kids, Christmas is supposed to be a *surprise*. It's no fun for the giver if it's not a *surprise*." She throws the model box on the floor and jams all her foot through the box and fragile plastic, twisting as if to put out a cigarette.

My brother and I gaze paralyzed at the crushed box.

"And I've told you and told you, you do not come into my room and go through my things." She picks up the record album. "I deserve—" she tears off the wrapper and pulls the record out of the sleeve—"some goddamn privacy"—she lifts the record over her head—"in my own goddamn house!"

In one move she lifts her knee, lowers the record, and smashes it in half.

Picking up each of the halves, she does it again.

She goes back into the closet and emerges with the USS Eisenhower and John Denver.

"Who touched this?"

Neither of us answers.

Eisenhower and Denver go down.

She goes back in.

"Last chance to tell me who the snoop is."

My eyes are stuck on shards of vinyl.

"That's it. I've had it. No Christmas for children who don't stay in their places."

A lavender blouse barely cooperates with being torn; a Matchbox 240Z proves invincible.

"Go to bed."

My brother and I walk quietly out, but shortly she's at the foot of our stairs again. "And another thing!" she bellows. "I felt the back of that TV set—it's hot. I know you were up watching TV—you're both grounded, two weeks!"

———

Here's all I will ever need to say about the suborned:

"God damn it!" I've been standing at the window by the front door watching until my mother's car leaves the curb, the dog tall next to me, paws on the windowsill. "What the fuck are you doing?" I hiss. "You're getting us in trouble! Now you've got me fucking grounded, you little shit!"

"I don't give a fuck about her and her stupid fucking rules," my brother says. Thirteen now, and destined to be 6'3", he's rail-thin like everyone in our family, but he's getting taller. He's broken 5', closing in on our mother and almost as strong as me. "You can fucking worship her and be a little kiss-ass and go along to her little school board meetings and cut out the articles when she's in the paper—and then turn around and kick *my* ass when I don't do things *her* way—I don't give a shit."

"You jerk. Do you want me to be grounded my entire fucking senior year? Anything you get, *I get*, you little shit."

"Come at me. Come on."

"I have actual *shit* going on in my life. I'm not some *loser*-load."

"Come on. I'm over here. You want me? Here I am."

"Do not turn that TV set on, you shit."

"Fuck you."

"Do not."

The dog collapses at the front door with a harrumph.

"Do not."

The dog watches us from between his elbows.

"Don't."

My brother settles into his spot on the floor in front of the tube.

"When she gets home, she's going to shove her stupid hands up the ass of that thing, and it's going to tell her how fucking long you were sitting in front of it, and that's it, I'm grounded for two weeks and I fucking miss the madrigals party."

My brother fastens his eyeballs on the screen. *Gunsmoke* blares its theme song.

It's two long strides for me to cross the room and plant my toes up his ass. In an instant he's up and I'm down, on my back, a pair of scissors at my throat.

I fight him off. He's got his weight on me. I fight.

"I told you come at me. What did you think I was saying?"

I fight.

"Cow. You're a fucking suckass everythingperfect straight-A neverintrouble BITCH." He lets me up. I leap to my feet.

I plant a decent jab on his upper arm.

"Come on," he says. He's laughing now. "Come at me."

I plant another.

"You got nothing," he says.

He sits back down on the floor.

I walk upstairs.

"You little FUCK!"

———

Which is not to say there weren't good times for the three of us.

———

My brother is not doing well in elementary school. The teacher calls my mother to say she's going to have to hold him back a year. He hasn't learned to read or write to grade level, and his behavior—he's a class distraction.

I'm nine, he's six. I don't know how long this goes on—forever, I think: we all three get home from school. Chores are done, supper is put on the table, supper is eaten, supper is cleaned up, I go upstairs.

From below I hear papers rustling. "OK," my mother says. "Make an A.

"Not like that. Like this.

"No, like *this*.

"No! A line this way, then that way. Then *cross*.

"OK. Make a B.

"OK. C.

"OK . . .

"No! Like this!"

There's a bang on the kitchen table. "Don't be stupid! Like this!

"*No*, and you will *not* play with me! That's *backward*—do it *again*!"

A thump. A cry. "That's *backward*! Do it *again*!"

A thump. Persistent whimper. "Again!"

Thump. Crying. "Again!"

Home. Supper served on kitchen table stacked with flash cards.

"Spell cat.

"OK. Spell dog."

I hear the dog's choke chain rattle. I know he's lifted his head, waited, put his head back down.

"OK. Spell lime.

"No. Spell *lime.*

"Spell sad.

"That's backward. Do it again.

"*Backward.* Again."

Bang. "You start this shit with me again and I swear to god I'll toss you on the street. Do it *right.*"

Thump. Cry.

"*Backward.* Do *not* play with me. I teach all day and then I come home to this shit. I'm in no mood. Do it *again.*"

I don't know how long it goes on, how many hours, how many weeks and months. It goes on forever.

In second grade my brother's IQ is tested, and my mother opens the report, looks at it, looks at it again. She calls the school. "Has there been a mistake?" she asks.

My brother sits blinking at me.

He's scored at the genius level—160-something.

He's diagnosed as hyperactive and learning disabled, and spends his childhood on Ritalin—when my mother can get him to take it. She tries to keep him from eating foods with the additives BHA and BHT, too, but the second he's off the school bus, his lunch money slides right into a vending machine.

Nobody has to tell me he's a fucking genius. I get interested in chess, need a partner, teach him the moves. First game we play ten minutes later, he kicks my ass. He spends twenty minutes with Risk, the board game, and global geography is eternally inked on frontal lobe. He won't do his homework, but he has *Jane's Fighting Ships* memorized cover-to-cover.

Upstairs, I can barely breathe, but downstairs at my mother's kitchen table, my brother learns to read and write.

———

In 1976, my junior year, my mother has been reelected president of her chapter, so she is president-elect when she, the president, and the negotiating team take the entire district out on strike that year.

She's *all over* the front page.

My brother and I enjoy a summer extended by three weeks. But we're entirely alone. She's in negotiations around the clock; some nights she gets in around four, sleeps a few hours, gets up, cleans up, heads for the picket lines. I sit on the steps by the bathroom as she applies mascara with a shuddering hand. "A teacher drinking coffee on the line was stung on the lip by a bee," she tells me. "The district just won't budge," she tells me. "The superintendent is still flirting with me," she says, "but he's not happy with me—he doesn't pat me on the butt anymore."

"Good," I say.

The phone rings off the hook. I pile up messages for her. She looks at them, sighs, walks away.

"They'll never respect us if we don't stand up to them," she says. "We have to stand together. It's like the secretaries. We can't get scared."

My mother has been trying to organize the district clerical staff. But they all work directly for management, and feel too vulnerable to unionize.

"Fucking management," my mother says—she's so tired she's not even hearing herself. "Lazay-fair is how they want it, right up till it costs them."

"Lazay-fair?" I say. "What's that?"

"Look it up," she says. "Hey," she says. "You know we're short for cash right now, right? Try to eat what we have here. Try to get by.

I'll pick up some milk and eggs tomorrow. You can make scrambled eggs. Scrapple and beans the night after. Then I don't know."

"I'll figure it out," I say.

I'm really proud of you, I don't say.

When we get back to school in late September, things settle down at school pretty quickly. But my mother isn't right. A searing neck pain, a nerve pinch maybe, goes on for two years; she doesn't sleep for ages; her stomach is off, she doesn't eat. Even in public she doesn't seem able to rebuild that scaffold, that face, that smile, laugh.

It's as if a truth settled on her shoulders, a mantle too heavy for the architecture that is her.

She'll teach for four more years, marry a guy with a little money, and retire in her late forties, cashing in her pension and investing it in a business with him. She'll lose the money, pack up, and move south. Rather than return to teaching, she'll become a Circle-K store clerk, and then a clerical worker in a courthouse.

I'll tell her about bullshit management moves I see going on at my university, and she'll sigh profoundly.

"Good god," she'll say. "It's the same even *there*. Good god."

———

When I leave for college, get the fuck out, launch, escape—not very far, only to the town where my mother's sister lives, where I have cousins, where the hills are—when I get out, it gets real bad. My brother's fourteen now.

My senior year had been tough for my mother and brother. My mother's old wedding rings end up buried in the back yard. A chunk of porcelain comes out of the sink. A lot of fights happen down the street.

After, I wasn't there. I'm so gone it doesn't even occur to me to wonder. I don't see it. I get a call on my dormitory room floor, my mother, telling me he's been arrested. She'd always said that when the cops got involved, she was through. She seems terrified—she's changed the locks and her phone number.

She's going to court to have him declared incorrigible.

"Where is he?"

Doesn't know, doesn't give a shit.

I scream, cry, beg. "Where is he?"

I gather coins, call my father from the hall pay phone. The girls on the hall slink silently past my panic. "Where is he?"

All my father knows is that he was arrested for shoplifting a pack of cigarettes.

"He's *smoking*?"

That's all he knows.

"You have to go get him."

He mumbles something.

"You have to go *get* him."

My father is finally, after thirteen years, remarried.

My mother has seen an opportunity. Clearly the timing of my brother's banishment is not coincidental.

I'm obsessed with where my brother is. He ends up in a detention hall of some kind, and then in a series of foster homes. Finally, my father takes him.

For a year, then, things are fine.

At the end of my sophomore year, my father tells me that because he now has to care for my brother, he will not be able to continue to contribute to my education.

"You have to sue him," my mother says.

"What?"

"All those years I did without—I mean *you* did without—so he could save for you—that's your money, you have to sue him."

I picture myself in a courtroom, on the witness stand, my father across from me.

"No," I say.

"Why not?"

"No."

"You have to!"

"No."

"All that hamburger we ate!"

"No."

"How do you expect to become a lawyer and stick up for other people when you won't even stick up for yourself?"

I already know I'm not headed for law school. The second I escape my mother, I toss flawless-daughterhood to the four winds. I discover the wonders of one of the oldest chemical processes know to humans: fermentation. I hook up with theater kids who spend all waking hours rehearsing, drinking, shouting about whether perfection in art is possible or even desirable. My grades are in the shitter and I'm ascending an exhilarating learning curve.

My mother is just now married for a third time, to a nice guy who leaps to her every command, and the two of them make me an utterly refusable offer: I can stay home and live with them and transfer to a local Penn State satellite. They'll buy me a car.

I'm finishing up what will be my last summer in the factory. That'll buy one semester if I live off campus cheap and eat a lot of Ramen noodles. I'm living in my mother's posh new house with her posh new nice husband and she's making me fucking miserable. I come home cowed from the factory, my back screaming from slouching over tile kits and grout machines, feet in what will turn out to be early stages of plantar fasciitis, lungs dehydrated from eight hours on the hundred-plus-degree floor. I'm nineteen. At school, I'm finally part of a scene, I'm doing something real (that, plus drinking), and I'm being forced to stretch, rise to the level of my challenging peers. What I have at last is the beginning of what will be *my life*. Not her fucking *psycho bullshit* idea of my life, tied to some stupid job I hate and taking it out on the world. Walking away from my own life would be suicide. Being back home this summer has been the first strangling rattle of death. I return from work at 3:00 wiped-out, grab a glass of water, choke out a "hi," walk upstairs, fall into my new posh bed, sleep till she hollers my name up the stairs, three times minimum, for what she now calls "dinner." I take a quick shower, run down.

I haven't helped put dinner together, I don't have anything scintillating to say at table, and—crime of crimes—I've left my water glass upstairs.

After supper I go upstairs and write letters to my drama friends at school.

In this posh house, the steps are carpeted, but, forever tough, she manages to effect a good pissed-off thump anyway. She soft-stomps into my room, sees the water glass. "What the hell is wrong with you? Why do you make me chase your trash all over the house? Bring the goddamn dirty glass downstairs when you're done with it. And don't even *think* about getting a water spot on this new furniture. This is the *guest* room now *too*, you know."

In nineteen years I've never known her to have a guest.

She grabs the glass from the nightstand, inches from my head. She hasn't hit me in two years, but I duck instinctively.

She stares at me. Stomps toward the door. "Oh," she says, turning for a perfect exit line, "it wouldn't kill you to lift one itty-bitty finger occasionally and help out around here. We're not here to wait on you hand and foot."

It had always been understood: *my brother was the problem*. Minus *him*, she and I would've been *fine*. Shrink after shrink *confirmed* this.

"Don't you understand?" she says to me finally. "We're newlyweds. We'd like to be alone occasionally. Why don't you ever leave the house?"

I don't have any friends around here. I didn't keep in touch with the few high school friends I did have—they were only coworkers, really, in my extra-curricular escape jobs. I don't have a car and now we live way out here. What was I going to do?

I refuse their generous offer.

"How are you going to get through school?" my mother demands.

"I'll figure it out," I say.

My father wants my brother to see his mother occasionally, and tells me to tell her this—he can't get her on the phone. I tell her and she flips. *FREAKS!* "Never! ever!" she yells, an unfamiliar desperation in her voice—"NEVER!"

I don't understand the depths of her terror—he was arrested for stealing a buck's worth of smokes, right? She shrieks at me. "If you *ever* give away my new number and address I'll NEVER SPEAK TO YOU AGAIN!"

And that, sad to say, is my greatest, secretest fear. That she will confirm, finally, what she's been performing right along: *she doesn't love me*.

I can see what's happening now. It happened to my mother's first husband. Shunning. When you're gone, you're gone. Never coming back again. Over my dead body. Don't even talk to me about him. Etc.

So I take a lesson from my mother. I tell my father that if he lets my brother phone the house, I'll never speak to him again.

I don't speak to my father for six years.

And when I go back to school that fall for my junior year, I never go home again. This means giving up the factory job—but who gives a flying fuck. I work two jobs during the school year, accumulate student debt, work three jobs during the summer, accumulate student debt.

Post-grad, in total poverty, I default on the student loans.

But fuck 'em *all*. Live free or fucking die.

———

When my mother becomes absorbed by union duties, I embrace as my personal theme song "Easy to Be Hard." The selection from *Hair*, my favorite among the rock musicals, perfectly articulates my mother's hypocrisy. "How can people be so heartless—especially people who care about strangers, who care about evil, social injustice—"

Hypocrisy is an obsession for those of us whose formative years take place in that massive, post-'60s hangover known as the '70s—Watergate only waters the full bloom of our outrage. At home, I've become the eco-pill. "You say you care about animals"—my mother is a pre-PETA save-the-seals freak, joining the World Wildlife Federation back when it's one guy and an inflated boat—"and you're using this *horrible* laundry detergent?" In this impersonal, planetary territory, I'm safe in scolding my mother. She takes my objections to heart and complies.

Easy to be hard.

"Do you only care about the bleeding crowd—"

Also, I'm studying voice and Three Dog Night's vocal arrangements never fail to kick ass, but on this 1969 track they outdo even themselves. Chuck Negron, he of the fab high tenor, in an age when high tenor is all the rage—Chuck hits that perfect E on "How," just at the edge of his range, a curvaceous, spherical tone, well supported. There's no reliance on the consonant—although "h" barely counts as a consonant in vocals; there's nothing there to launch you—he simply rings the "ow" right out of his diaphragm, jes' like he's ringin' a bell. Then he descends into the lower octave, closer to the center of his range, right where the broad tones live, right where songwriters MacDermot-Rado-Ragni want him to go, right where the furies are, throat-singing "heartless."

I play it 972 times, head cradled in the gentlest of hands, my earphones. The helplessness of the how, the wrath of the heartless.

3.

My second year in college, I start writing stories again, and one of the first ones I write is the one about my grandparents, the one I'll win the award for at graduation, about how they live in the mountains, jousting each other with their hatred.

My mother is the only one in the family I show the story to. My mother has said, You're a good writer.

She's not given to praise.

The one and only string my mother pulls when I attend her high school is to get me enrolled, as a sophomore, in a creative writing class open only to seniors. One day the teacher troops down to my mother's classroom.

She writes like Hemingway, he says.

Spring break. My mother and I are alone now, my brother with my father. I give my mother the story. I give my mother the story in the middle of the evening, when my mother will be at the kitchen table writing in her journal.

Second beer.

I wait upstairs.

When I write the story, I imagine what it would have been like: I think about the babies my grandmother had back-to-back, each a year apart during the Depression, in the middle of nowhere, sealed off by impervious Appalachian ridges. I remember the stories my grandmother told about begging, how humiliating it was—milk for the children, please—her husband traipsing through the woods with his rifle, bringing back the odd squirrel, rabbit, deer on a good day—these stories in which a mountain is food—these stories are truth, true or not. For years I listened to my mother complain end-lessly, not about hunger, but about being the one responsible for breaking the necks of chickens—the horror of it. Her father can't bring himself to do it, so she does it. I imagine how someone might feel about desperate hillside poverty and pregnancies and the urgent needs of tiny babies. In my story, when it happens the fourth year in a row, the husband beats up the wife for being pregnant again.

My grandfather wouldn't hurt a fly. I don't know where I got the notion that he might slap his wife. It isn't a guess so much as a spec-ulation, an imagining.

I wait upstairs. Pages rustle. It's a familiar sound—my mother reading papers composed by her forty-hour-a-week-factory-work-ing-car-owning-I'm-just-here-for-a-fucking-high-school-diploma students-who-are-not-students.

Pages rustle.

I look at my nails. My mother keeps her nails long and paints them twice a week. So do I. The smell of acetone is not uncommon in our house.

My cuticles could use some work.

Pages rustle.

A glass is picked up and put back down.

I walk downstairs and lurk in the dark dining room. My mother sits at the kitchen table with the story in front of her, smoke curling high, the fingers of one hand around a can of Carling Black Label.

She is crying, her head low, her other hand holding her forehead.

I've never seen my mother cry.

"What's wrong!" I say.

My mother looks up at me and wipes her eyes.

"How did you know?" she says.

———

By the time I'm in college, my aunt has talked my grandparents into moving to town, where she can help them more, keep an eye on their health. They sell the mountain place and buy a trailer in a park on the edge of town, where I visit them once a week.

It's a disaster. Cigarette cartons, Gainesburgers, ashtrays, seashells, leashes, magazines, bills, receipts, stained grocery lists, split bags of hard candy, dusty tissue boxes, wadded tissues, *TV Guide*. Their beagle's hair matted everywhere. The bathroom a mess of sticky misses.

I'm responsible for cleaning it but I'm not much for responsibility these days, except to my theater pals. I don't move all the stuff. I dust around things, or rather through things, dust the half-inch space between things, run the vacuum over the rugs—interstices, not space but spaces between space. At my grandmother's insistence I lift the upright vacuum cleaner—no attachments—onto the couch and run it over the cushions in a feeble attempt to get the dog hair off. They don't seem to have much laundry, but I throw a small load into the miniature, stacked Kenmore in the back of the trailer while I putter around. Basically, I clean for the length of time it takes to get one load washed, out of the dryer and folded.

I do a decent job in the bathroom, which is the thing my grandfather cares most about. I spray it head to foot with Dow and wipe up the foam, trying not to breathe. I elbow-grease the goddamn bathtub, one of those plastic numbers that won't let crud go no matter what the hell you spray on it or rub it with.

My grandfather has the twenty fresh and ready. I need it. I'm out of Wild Turkey and that'll almost cover my binging—liberation via libation. We sit and drink his cheap bourbon when I should be studying political philosophy. Locke, Hobbes—can't keep the motherfuckers straight—Nietzsche, the end of god, Hegel, the end of narrative history. The three of us sit on a couch, slap at the fleas, watch TV and compete for the beagle's affection, macerating in the vinaigrette that is my grandparents' mutual rage, the only thing we all truly share.

———

I call my aunt and tell her I'm afraid to tell my mother that I'm failing Latin. "If I'm lucky," I say into the dormitory pay phone, "the guy will let me go with a D."

"He's such a jerk," I whine.

My aunt is comforting. "Your mother will understand," she says. "She knows what that snobby school is like—they're overworking you there. Latin is incredibly hard. And you know, it's completely ridiculous too." My aunt may have flunked out of nursing school, but as a swim coach and aerobics instructor, she knows more about anatomy, nutrition, and sports medicine than a lot of nurses. "I flunked Latin too, and you really don't need Latin to do anything. They tell you you need it, but you really don't."

I *had* thought I needed it for law school. "Malarkey," she says. "Do they speak Latin in court? No. So don't worry about it. I'm sure you did the best you could."

Well, actually, I hadn't. But I *did do* the best I *cared* to do.

"Come on out for dinner tonight and forget about it. I'll send the boys to pick you up. That is, unless you've got a date with one of the snobs."

We both laugh at the impossibility of this, and then hang up. I dash downstairs when I hear the usual honk. I climb into my cousin's Dart and breathe deeply of that familiarly fabulous old-car smell.

My mother is furious. "A *D* in Latin?" she demands. "What the hell's wrong with you?"

"I did the best I could," I say, waiting for that understanding thing to kick in.

"Bullshit," she barks. "What you did was earn yourself a kick in the ass. How can you even think about law school with grades like this?"

"Peg says that you don't really need Latin anyway," I protest.

"I don't give a shit what Peg says. Peg doesn't know shit about colleges. You'll be just like her, flunking out of school. And you be careful with her—she always wants what I have."

In truth, it's plain to me that my aunt is competing with my mother for my affections. Peg seems to think she knows what I need better than my mother does. Peg thinks my mother is too hard on me. Peg thinks my mother has problems with depression. Peg bakes my favorite birthday cake: chocolate with peanut butter icing. My mother never baked a cake in her life.

———

None of my mother's siblings did the college thing—in which college becomes job training—and neither did the cousins of my generation, and neither did my brother: some precedent for me, then, thanks to my parents. My mother's oldest brother went to work for the nearby military supply depot, as his father had also eventually done, and made good money with no education, by typing stuff—"programs"—into newfangled things called computers. My mother's younger brother started a drinking and woman-battering and breaking-and-entering career, requiring regular bailouts. Until the incident that landed him in the state pen. The incident no one could bail him out of.

This uncle, who was around a lot—no job, I guess—was my favorite when I was a kid. His trailer is a mile down the road and he picks up me and my brother and we drive to Cowan's Gap with his two sons. Where is his wife? Working in her family's business. Bringing in a paycheck. Once in the lake, shiny browngreen impenetrable, he ducks underwater, places our feet on his shoulders and then rises from the water—a giant monster!—and between him pushing and us jumping he tosses our damn butts halfway across the lake in a careening splash. I haven't mastered the whole thing about diving into water without getting a snootful—*always be exhaling!*—and I come up sputtering. "Well, ya dumb bunny," my uncle says. That's his nickname for me. Dumb Bunny. "Ya forgot ta hold yer nose, ya dumb bunny." He smacks my shoulder blades as I cough up lake and mountain. On the way home he follows me across the sand and picks up what I absentmindedly leave behind. My brother and cousins race across the creek that's been dammed to make the lake, tear over a forest floor of pine needles and stones *how calloused are their magnificent feet* while my chin pokes a book. "God damn it, ya forgot yer stupid towel, ya dumb bunny. Jest slow down for a damn minute. All these summer school ecology classes you volunteer for, wanting to be so smart, and you can't remember your damn towel."

Verdict: assault with a deadly weapon, attempted murder. Of his wife. His paycheck.

———

When my grandfather retires from his government job, he moves his wife permanently onto Tuscarora Mountain. He and his sons and son-in-law build on a modest addition to the tiny trailer, as well as a small separate building. It's cramped and run-down, but to the grandkids it's heaven. As young teens, my brother and I hang out with delinquent boys who live up the road ("Who are their people?" my grandmother asks suspiciously), helping my grandfather dam the creek down the hill so we'll have a pool to soak our feet in, throwing our leftovers behind the trailer to feed the deer, playing 31 for pennies around the kitchen table with my youngest uncle and his boys, taking the spotlight that plugs into the cigarette lighter and, come evening, spotting for deer down in the valley, sitting between my grandfather's knees in the car for driving lessons, steering the ancient Plymouth into a tree and cringing—waited to get whacked but good—knee-slapping laughter instead—was he sober?—splashing around at the Gap, pretending to fish with my grandfather in his aluminum rowboat—

—he complains because I always make him throw the sunnies back, and I eat all the bait—Colby cheese warmed by sun—the only bait I'll let him use—

—nothing like it—

"I was afraid he'd hit me," I tell my grandmother.

"He wouldn't hurt a fly," she replies idly.

My grandfather and I have only one disagreement. During my visits, we stage a running, years-long, never-ending battle about whether I will be allowed to read. I insist on bringing all of my library books with me, and he sneaks up behind me and snatches them out of my hands. "You're on vacation!" he hollers.

"But I want to read," I say.

"No you don't," he says, and makes a face, holding the book out of my reach. "Go play."

I stand there helplessly. "Give me the book back!"

"Go play! Get some fresh air!"

"I want to read!"

"You can't learn common sense from a book. You always have your damn nose in paper. Now get out there and learn something else, you want to learn so much."

"Leave her alone," my grandmother says from the next room with little conviction. "She's a smart kid. Let her read."

"She's too bookish!" he yells, then turns his attention to a fight with the old woman while I scamper off. In the distance, his voice talking about how dumb I can be, how clumsy, how I lack common . . . his voice follows after me. I wait till he's busied himself with watering his flowers, or spreading gravel on the drive, or piling up charcoal, and hunt around till I find where he's hidden my book. Take it and hide somewhere in the trees, down over a rise where he can't see. Dry leaves scratch my skin and I settle in, find my lost place.

———

My grandmother is in the hospital. I'm supposed to call my aunt right away. My college roommate doesn't know anything else.

I'm a senior, trying to get an English major together while not at the same time flunking the time-sucking theater courses I had signed up for before deciding last-minute to switch to English—I'm in college—a top-tier, before I know what a tier is, liberal-arts school, very posh—the college in my aunt's town, the alleys of which I have raced up and down in—I'm in college with that major change of major going on, when this happens. My grandparents are just back from their trailer in Florida, and spring has been late in coming this year. *Spring was late in coming this year.* I get home exhausted from a rehearsal one night, from a rehearsal of the last show I'll ever do in college, from a rehearsal of my last musical ever—*Candide*—when this happens.

My roommate sits me down in that uh-oh-serious way to tell me that my aunt, who lives about a mile from campus with my uncle and two favorite cousins—my roommate sits me down to tell me that my aunt called.

You're supposed to call her right away.

My roommate doesn't know anything else. Well versed in keeping my mouth shut, I haven't told anyone at college about my grandmother. I don't tend to mention my family at all. I maintain two lives, keep two separate peaces. I live here, one mile from the library, I live there, five miles out on the edge of town in the trailer park near the quarry.

Dos vidas. Zwei Standzeiten.

I grab something to inhale—slice up a hard-boiled egg and slather some white bread with mayonnaise and layer the slices and salt the shit out of it and eat it with a beer that actually belongs to my roommate. Jane, pre-law and From Money, keeps her stuff on the right side of the fridge and I keep mine on the left. But Jane can tell something's up that's not good so she doesn't object when I ask if I can borrow a beer. Maybe more than one for that matter. But this isn't the only reason it takes me a while to make the call.

My grandmother has twice traveled to twenty-eight-day detox farms to dry out from prescription drugs and booze. My mother and aunt pay for it, far as I know. It doesn't quite do it. As far as they know, although my grandfather claims otherwise, she finally quits with the uppers (in the morning) and the booze (late afternoon)—but that leaves her in a state the shrinks call "dry drunk." She trades one addiction for another. And this one is scary. Whenever she gets panicky—and no one ever asks her *why* she gets panicky—she stops eating. Then she "gets sick" with some unidentifiable illness and the doctor sticks her in the hospital and runs a zillion tests that come back negative and she stumps medical science. When all they have to do is say to her, "For god's sake, woman, eat something."

And I try not to think about the fact that my middle-aged aunt and mother are both thin. Quite thin. I've never known my mother not to be on some kind of diet or another.

I'm thin too.

When I get old, I will be fat, I pledge to myself. Big and fluffy and roly-poly.

But of course, that won't solve the real problem, any more than would the drug farms.

When I finally call, too late for my aunt to want to talk long, my aunt tells me that this time they put my grandmother in the psych ward.

This is a first.

The doctors are catching on, I think to myself. "She can't have visitors yet," my aunt says. "But we're going to go see her on Friday. One of the boys will pick you up."

"I have rehearsal," I quickly lie, without thinking. Of course no college student, no matter how dedicated to her art, rehearses on Friday nights, second only to Saturday as the most important drinking night of the week. But it takes me only a split second to know that I can count on my aunt's not knowing this. I ask how my grandfather is doing.

"He's fine," my aunt says. "He's coming here for dinner tomorrow."

"I'll go see him in the morning," I say. "Make sure he's OK."

"That would help a lot," my aunt says.

Friday evening, when I know they'll be finished at the hospital and my grandfather will be alone, I borrow Jane's car and drop by the trailer to mix highballs and watch TV with him, discuss who shot J.R. I ask him how he's feeling. He seems fine.

I try to ignore an observation about a man I adore. But: he seems almost—satisfied.

My aunt calls to say my grandmother is doing better. "She's just a little out of it from the sedation. But you can go see her anytime now." She rattles off the visiting hours. I mumble something about midterms keeping me busy.

I try to get over to the trailer for supper, make sure he's eating OK. I have papers due and have to rush things a bit with him. "I have tons of reading to do," I tell him as I toss spaghetti with Prego and put out the green can of Parmesan cheese. "You and your books," he grumbles for the nine-hundredth time. "You read too much. Bad for your eyes." He has glaucoma, kneads his brows just thinking about it. "I have rehearsals to deal with too," I say. Theater seems to work better as an excuse. They don't know what I do there, and they don't come to my shows. It doesn't occur to me to invite them. But I think they think that theater is at least . . . doing something. Whereas reading and writing are . . . nonproductive? I'm not sure what they think—I don't ask. This time out, though, it really *is* midterms and I really *have* become, finally, interested in this weird, nothing-major they vaguely term English, and I really *do* have to finish a paper on reflexive gestures in *Tristram Shandy* and *Moby-Dick*—so I don't really clean the place, just wipe around things and put his laundry in the miniature stacked washer. "You'll have to take it out of the dryer and fold it, OK?"

He seems more relaxed than usual, pushes the usual twenty on me, and I take it with greater reluctance than usual. I know I'm robbing them and they don't have much. But for him this is affection, caring. And I don't have much either and now I owe Jane a six-pack.

He doesn't tell me how my grandmother is doing, and I don't ask. My grandparents don't get along well. They snark at each other all day long. About nothing.

My cousin tells me she's looking better and better. "I'll take you over," he says.

"After I get through rehearsals," I say. "I'm TD-ing this show. *Candide*. Christ. I have to figure out a way to hang a guy without actually hanging a guy."

My cousin has no response to this.

Jane doesn't ask why I'm gone so often at suppertime these days and why I keep borrowing her car. I never tell her what my grandmother is in for.

My grandmother is in the psych ward. The place where white-trash crazy people like her go. Not a place for not-quite-first-generation white-trash readers of—well, by now we're on *The Sound and the Fury*. Weeks have gone by. I really do have to go visit. "She's doing really well," everyone says. "We'll take you over."

Weeks have gone by. The hospital is two, maybe three miles from campus, but I can't bear the thought of asking for Jane's car again. And I can't bear the thought of being fetched out of my slum-end-of-town apartment in my cousin's thundering '66 Dodge Dart chariot, the black guy next door frowning from his stoop at our unmuffled whiteness. My cousins being redheads and all. Carrot-topped freckle-faced where'd-you-put-the-fucking-sunscreen whiter-than-white folk, on our way to the fucking loony bin, which is where *we're* all going to end up, every single last moley-freckled one of us.

I don't have to tell you, right? Why I don't want to do this? My grandmother is one of precisely two people who have been good to me just because we share the same stupid Pennsylvania Dutch-ish—a bit of Scots-Irish, a fair dollop of Mennonite—blood, without asking anything back. And my grandmother's a goddamn so-called recovered drunk and pill-popper and how am I supposed to explain that to my theater friends, the drama fags, my writing friends, the scribble hags, the people reading Edward Albee and making a beer game of who's most afraid of Virginia Woolf. If you made it halfway through *Mrs. Dalloway*, take a sip. If you finished it, take two sips. If you think you *understood* it, take three. This way, the smarter you are, or the more full of shit you are, the drunker you get.

On a belatedly nice spring day, I walk it.

The street I take leads through the affluent neighborhood, an area where I know a few of my professors and a lot of local business executives have homes. My uncle's boss at the trucking company lives there. The lawns are ample and fresh, the houses stately and mute.

I look at the vast and vacant green and think about the black guy next door, ever on his stoop.

What is it about rich people that you never see them outside?

At the front desk, I ask where my grandmother is. The woman consults a printout. "Fourth floor."

Off the elevator, the floor is locked. Another woman sits at another desk outside a wide door, closed, clenched, with one small window. While the woman looks up my grandmother's name, I peer through the glass. A large room is furnished with couches scattered in no specific arrangement. People in blue dressing gowns sit quietly with people in street clothes. Other blue-gowned people surround an elevated TV.

I don't like the sour smell. It's a prison we're in—my grandmother is shut in, she's "in stir," as they say in old gangster films, she's penned in, and if I'm not careful with my stupid one-half-white-trash ass, if I don't do what I'm told, if I go down the wrong road in a bellowing '66 Dodge Dart, they'll nab me too.

The woman takes me in. My grandmother slumps on a couch, staring out the window, the customary crumpled Kleenex in her lap. I'm surprised. I'm accustomed to finding her in front of a noisy TV. At home, she scours the game shows, especially *Hollywood Squares* and *Jeopardy*. She shouts the answers. When she gets a lot of them right, I tell her she's really smart. "Skipped second grade, kid," she says every time. "Got a perfect attendance medal when I graduated high school."

It's important to my grandmother that I understand that when she married my grandfather, who attended school only until the sixth grade, she married down. Beneath herself. *She* has been *educated*. *She* reads *Redbook* cover to cover every month. Can this marriage be . . .

"I should have been a teacher," she says to me one day.

"You would've been a good one," I say. "You are a good one."

"Teachers should be people who actually want to be doing it."

I nod.

But, like the rest of my family, she expresses no real interest in my education, except to ask me repeatedly what sort of job I think it's going to lead to. "This theater stuff," she says. "What's that going to get you?" "Yeah," my grandfather says. It's one of the few points on which they agree.

"Hello," my grandmother says in a friendly, formal tone. "Sit down," she says. Her smile is distant, but sincere.

"Howya been?" I ask, as if we've run into each other at the liquor store.

It's been known to happen.

"Oh, I've been better, kid," she says in her teasing voice. "But I'm doing quite well, thank you for asking. How's school?"

"Fine."

"You look flushed," she says, and then looks away from me, toward the window. "You're studying too hard."

"I walked."

"You should've had one of the boys drive you," she says.

We sit there. Outside the window, the gray trees bud, and tulips emerge sturdy and vibrant. Squirrels hound each other and birds flap to and fro, assembling a place for this year's eggs.

All of life seems purposeful. All but the life lived in this room.

I would never do this. How could you do this? I would never want to extinguish myself and don't understand why you keep insisting. Insisting. That's what a writer once said: repetition isn't repetition—it's insistence.

"Look," my grandmother says. "There's a robin. I guess it's finally spring."

But then . . . another writer says repetition is also delay. Tristram's nasal tale neglecting to arrive at the story of his birth, intensifying, by stalling, our gratification.

"I believe it *is* spring," I say. "Again."

But then . . . still another writer: repetition can't by definition be repetition, since what repeats may be sameness but not identicalness.

"It'll be good to see another summer," my grandmother says.

Delay. Sameness. Insistence.

Insistence on sameness delayed.

Your contradictions are too obvious, I don't say. You *want* to see another summer while working to *deny* yourself another summer.

We sit looking out the window, not touching. I want to take one of the hands that lie idly in my grandmother's lap, cupped around the Kleenex, but the woman looks too thin, too frail in the blue gown that swallows her. We sit instead and watch the squirrels and the robins. We sit for a long time and I realize that I will have to get up soon and walk back across town to campus. But I cannot imagine leaving. Indeed, I cannot imagine the campus. There are limits, to imaginings. In this room, with this woman who has done everything she could for me simply because we are related—an attitude I barely comprehend—with this woman, the world of that campus, those gray bricks, those revered buildings, is too far-flung. I can't conjure a reason to argue about Gödel's second incompleteness theorem, and its impact, if any, on theories of interpretation. I can't conceive of the urgency of ferreting out ideological state apparatuses. I can't seem to get past page three of *Ulysses* and don't know why I must experience Dublin in that way. I don't understand the problem of mimesis, and find sixties theater increasingly absurd. I don't remember why I am here. *There*, I mean. These linguists, going on and on about t-r-e-e not being that thing out there on which the robins perch. What was that theory guy talking about in 1968, a mere twelve years prior to this moment, in a language I don't understand? Something about the author dying, an author being after all only a convenience invented by critics to limit the possible meanings of a text—this before he wrote his autobiography. What was that other theory guy talking about in 1969, a mere eleven years prior to this moment? Something about "the author function" being a cultural construct that changes with economic circumstance and institutional organization. Institutional. Organization. *That's* an institution—*there*—and *this* is an institution—*here*. The more time I spend *there*, and the more I go *there* by way of attempting to escape *here*, the farther away—the point is too obvious to bother with, really—*the farther away I get from here.*

Or such was the plan.

Why would she do it? You stop eating, tissue dies. Brain cells fade. Skin snuffs. Liver cramps. Pancreas creams. The heart pumps madly, striving to distribute less and less nourishment to organs needing more and more. I would never do this. I can't imagine doing this. Where is it she thinks she's going from here? If here is too awful to eat for, if she cannot swallow *here*, what does she think comes after the consumption stops? After the heart gives up on her and tells her to go fuck herself, it's done working overtime, she can find herself another patsy to slave away for her, what then? What is her *there*? Where is she going?

In fact, the only theorist of any use to me at this moment is the guy who leads the funereal procession for binary oppositions, of which, and I oversimplify, I am the walking dead, the walking seated, the walking collapsed. Gown maintains itself as gown simply by not being town, gown requiring town for its very existence, town serving as the thing gown is not and refuses to be, gown wondering in fact where it would be were town not there to perform as relief, town not requiring gown at all but unifying in resistance to gown, town finding that amalgamation to be a useful side effect of gown's arrogance, town collecting itself to tell gown to fuck off, town getting in its pickups and '66 Dodge Darts and cruising on Friday nights, town not sitting in the bars and fraternity houses with gown (tried that once, foolishly, flannelled cousin nearly in fistfight with dockered supercilious), town instead drinking from six-packs tucked under empty rifle racks, cruising, circling and circling an eight-block area, over and over, two blocks turn left two blocks turn left two blocks turn left two blocks turn left *why do we never turn right* around and around and where it stops nobody knows, town gaping at gown, town shouting insults at gown, town *boys* in particular whistling insults (though some take them as compliments) at gown *girls*, town asleep at the wheel as gown passes out on quad, gown requiring town so gown will know for certain what it is that gown doesn't even have to *try* to escape, town not needing gown except to coalesce, to channel the antipathy—

—then too, there's the black guy next door. A different town entirely?

My grandmother and I sit looking out the window, not touching,

Kleenex undisturbed, until they come and take her away for a dinner that's probably not very good in the first place, not near as good as her own pork chops for instance—her pork chops—and here I feel forced to use an unfortunate expression—her pork chops are to die for—but in the second place, the orderly will stand over her and make her eat it, make of her plate a contested site. I know precisely the treatment the orderly is in for, because I've suffered through it myself. While you sit there, head on palm, the woman will push the food around delicately with her fork, take a tiny bite and chew it daintily forfuckingever—table manners being very important to her and a lady never hangs her head over her plate and stuffs her mouth like a hog—a lady never eats as if she is actually hungry—yet from her acts of starvation we conclude that she is wholly and entirely famished—and you'll say, "Eat, Helen, come on for chrissake," and she'll say, in her formal, I-married-beneath-myself tone, "I *am* eating, if you please"—and—just to piss you off—just to maintain some power of her fucking *own*—just to keep control of her own fucking life—"Watch your language, please"—she'll make you sit with her at the table, a small kitchen table cluttered with bills and checkbooks and Medicare paperwork and god knows what-all else you had to shove aside to make just enough room for three plates—she'll keep you there long after he has lurched up with his bad knees and said, "Don't bother yourself, the hell with her," and gone over to sit in front of the TV—his after-supper preferences running toward old reruns like *The Fugitive*—she'll keep you there until after an hour she's eaten about half of it *maybe* and finally you'll give up, cry uncle, carry the plate and fork to the trash and swab the bones and dump the plate and fork in cold dishwater, soap suds all gone, soap suds all having exhausted their capacity for bubbles, the plate and fork the last thing to be washed before you leave and go back to the library where you belong *where waits the writer who is afraid of dying before the end of a long sentence—*

Because the thing that's going on here is what my grandfather did to my grandmother, and mother, a long, long time ago. And my grandparents gave me my mother, but my mother gave me my grandparents. Uncomfortable herself, she nonetheless did us the great favor of dropping us off. Kicking down that dirt road. Letting the games begin.

Oh yeah, I know all about dinner with my grandparents, him with head suspended over plate elbows on table mouth wide open false teeth gnashing breaded seared baked pork. "How's school?" he says, tongue pushing pork aside. "Fine," I say—have I used the phrase white trash? Trailer trash? He'll want me to mix highballs for the two of us later. Three ice cubes per glass. First one finger of bourbon, then two, then three, all the drinking tightly scheduled, first at nine, second at nine-thirty, third at nine-forty-five—medicinal—in his case, to treat knee pain—my grandmother sober and supposedly recovered and looking a bit disdainful as we indulge— then bedtime and I drive home one-third tanked already—we hold our liquor well in this family—when I give the car back to Jane and hit the fraternities. Me, I'm town *and* gown, the keeled-over binary, cruiser *and* drama-fag frat-hag, a walking Mason-Dixon line, a seceding union, a Gettysburg (not far from here), a position of opposition. Me, I'm town and gown, white and half-trash (first generation on my mother's side), and I do not belong. And this woman loves me entirely because I am Eyler and Wolford, another site of opposition, kind of like if Romeo and Juliet had lived to get married and fifty years later found themselves gnawing pork chops with false teeth in a trailer at the edge of town near the limestone quarry that you hear and smell all day, five miles from that charming, eighteenth-century, tuition-prohibitive place of higher learning con-structed entirely of local—well, we all know what it was built of. Not a day of school she missed, or so she rehearses it. Skipped the second grade and gets half the questions on *Jeopardy* entirely cor-rect. And Gödel, don't you know, he starved himself to death too. And for a few weeks now I haven't performed my usual half-assed job of sort-of cleaning their trailer for the twenty bucks my grand-father stuffs at me, and when he gives me the twenty bucks I spend it mostly on booze, after he and I get sloshed on highballs made of bottom-shelf gallon-jugged bourbon, and I know that goddamned plastic bathtub of theirs which never comes clean probably needs scrubbed real bad by now, and he could probably use a bourbon buddy. And the woman's in here for drinking and pill-popping and not eating, and we're out there, drinking—me so much that two in the morning finds me with head dallying over basin or maybe it's four in the morning head dangling behind bumper. And I am town and gown but here, sitting on a couch in a psych ward where the woman has dropped the damn Kleenex on the floor as she stands and leaves—"So long, kid"—she is town and all that matters *here* is that I am town.

Not least because I'm about to graduate in the bottom ten per-cent of my class, and when I do, I'm not going to have the money to move away from here. My first Adult Job will be in theater here, administrator and producer of a teaching ballet company.

So *there*, fuckers. The goddamn drama shit got me someplace after all.

Here, I do not watch as the woman walks slowly away, stooped, she was always stooped, she skipped the second grade and is the smartest person I know, or so I rehearse it—skipped the second grade and is the smartest person I know—or so I rehearse it—but now she is not in second grade, and is not the smartest person I know—she loves me entirely because I am Eyler and Wolford (she skips past the Fleisher part)—but now she is a stooped and spent and slight old woman, with much the same blood but not the self-same blood, she having birthed my mother and my mother having birthed me but *I* having birthed *neither* of *them*, she stooping on the arm of the white-coated stranger, the orderly, who will be much more stubborn than I, I'm sure, about making sure she swallows. All of it.

———

Two years after I graduate, my younger cousin gets a young girl pregnant and a hasty wedding is convened. And, my aunt shuns me. *You're such a snob, you think you're so much better than us because you went to that snobby school and now you hold it over all of us—I don't want my kids around you—you stay away from us! We don't need you and your kind!*

My aunt holds the annual birthday party for my grandfather. I'm not invited, and my grandparents comply with this. My cousins are forbidden to talk to me, and they comply with this.

I'm dead.

My grandparents die some months later, while staying in their Florida trailer. Ten years after that, my uncle makes a passing reference to the service the family held to remember them. I wasn't invited. I was dead.

———

When I graduate with my Ph.D.—from a high-second-tier institution—my father attends the ceremonies. My stepmother—high school and one year business school, no college—has theater tickets with her daughter—Penn State, accounting—and can't make it. I'm bummed but I'm not allowed to say so.

My brother hasn't been speaking to me for some years. Dead again.

I had called my mother a month prior, having passed a milestone—a meeting with my dissertation director at which he told me that the final draft was fine, that he'd be asking for no revisions at my dissertation defense. They always ask for revisions and I'm hugely relieved—although I've always suspected that he didn't have a chance to read the final draft, busy as he was with family problems.

"I made it," I told my mother. "I'm through. I can't believe it."

Really thought I might not. Make it. Didn't think I could write a novel, pass all those exams, get through all those courses, fill all the "gaps" in my reading left by my fourth-tier master's degree—AND do it in three years, the sum total of time, or so I had closely— closely—calculated, that my divorce settlement ($7,000) would provide for.

"Oh!" my mother says. "Well listen, you know I'm not coming up for this, right?"

"What?" I say.

"To your college graduation. I can't come up. I have to take care of the cats, and the dog hasn't been doing well, and I just can't travel right now."

I hold the phone in my hand. A familiar sensation descends.

College. She insists on calling it *college.* When I told her I was going to do writing seriously, that I was going to go to grad school if I could find one that would forgive my undergraduate record, she said, "What do you need more *college* for?"

"I haven't even thought about graduation. I'm just calling to say I'm shocked I made it."

"Oh, OK," my mother says. "Maybe you could come down sometime and we'll make you a graduation party here!"

I hold the phone in my hand. What she wants me to do is say, as I have done for decades, Sure, all right, it's OK if you don't come to my graduation—I'll agree to some ridiculous compensation prize that will never happen because I don't know a fucking soul down there except you and Mr. Nice—

"Sure," I lie. "All right." I hold the phone in my hand. "That would be nice," I lie.

"You're not going to use the title, are you?" my mother says.

"Excuse me?"

"The title. 'Doctor.' I hate it when people do that—so snobbish."

Familiar sensation.

"No, no, of course not," I say.

When I accepted my teaching assistantship three years prior, I signed a piece of paper saying that teaching my one course per semester—for $8,000 per nine months plus tuition waiver—would be the only job I would take. But I can't—am not permitted, due to undergrad loan default—to borrow—and—and this next part was all my own decision—I also don't want to downscale my lifestyle. I'm no longer the youngest in my class: I'm starting my Ph.D. at the age of thirty-one. I've been in the world. I own things—divorce detritus—and I hire a moving van to deliver them. I want my own place and don't want it to be a piece of shit student slum *and* am only just discovering a nasty truth about college towns: rentals are high. Landlords milk students who are willing to bunk two to a room and partition rent four ways. If you don't want to rent in the educational ghetto, you pay, and high. So I'd gotten another job adjuncting at a community college, and still another, teaching country western dance classes in VFW halls and bars—this in the boom years, the "Achy Breaky Heart" era. So. *Dos vidas*. One foot in intellectual boot camp, the other in underclass, underkempt, undereducated, overly Old-Spiced anti-intellectualism. The left foot doesn't know what the right foot is doing, even as they smoothly two-step.

"Adjunct": "attached in a subordinate or temporary capacity to a staff," says *Merriam-Webster's*.

So my father, bless him, comes up—three-hour drive—for my graduation—the first time in my life I am truly proud of an accomplishment. And there's this one cool thing I groove on. There are thousands of students getting degrees that day, most of them baccalaureates, but the only people who walk up on the stage are the people receiving Ph.D.'s. When we get on the stage, the president of the university hands us our diplomas and shakes our hands. Then we step before the dean of the graduate school, who "hoods" us—drapes around our necks the "hood" bearing the school colors. It's all just terribly *Hahvahd*. Afterwards, when the faculty gets up and begins the procession out, the Ph.D. recipients rise and follow them, symbolizing our having joined their ranks. I get totally cranked by this shit.

Side note: The hand I shake, and the hands that robe me, are both, that year, the hands of women. As I accept my fake diploma—the real one is gratification-delayed in the mail—I say (a bit loudly, to be heard over the applause), "It's so cool to see women up here!"—

—and the owner of those hands looks at me blankly. But never mind. I have more important concerns as I walk toward the dean. I don't wear dresses, but I bought a dress for the occasion, and queen-size pantyhose (I don't gain my freshman-fifteen until I do my Ph.D. comps), and new shoes—and the goddamn shoes—I must have bought them late in the day or something—are skid-slipping off my fucking heels. I'm lucky to get off the fucking stage without breaking my fucking back.

From the stage and from my seat, I look everywhere for my father. Can't find him. But still. He's there.

On my father's visits he likes nothing more than to hang out at the roadhouse where I've been teaching dance—which enjoyment I've anticipated—no-brainer—he's a daily pub visitor—so we spend some time out there. It's at this same roadhouse that I'll hold my graduation party, attended by my closest dancing and roadhouse buddies.

Friends? Well, the word would have to do too much work if I used it. Buddies. That'll do.

The buddies show up with grocery-store shrimp cocktail platters and cheese plates while my boss serves draft beer on the house, an out-and-out abandonment of his No Such Thing As A Free Beer policy. People (there are about a dozen) bring the usual graduation cards, some with twenties inside—but a twenty is something to these folks, and to their mind it's the thing to do, even if I am thirty-three—and a fuss is made for a few minutes and my closest buddy tells me how proud she is of me, and several cans of Silly String are distributed and for another five minutes grown men and women run about spurting aerosolized chemical compounds in each other's faces and then—

—that's that. NASCAR gets turned on and folks settle in at the bar to watch Dale (car #3, and thanks to running around to central PA racetracks with my cousin I know a little something about racing) and drink free beer.

They don't get what's happening. I hate to say it but I guess I must, even if wincingly: I love them, but the people from your second life are not the best people to ask to help celebrate your first life. I have, as advised, gone on the academic job market as an ABD (all but dissertation finished, all but dead, alive but decaying, always be dumbest), and come up zero. Bageled it. At this point I have no idea that a game is being played, and that I don't have a copy of the rulebook. Or, machinery is operating and I don't have the instruction manual. After graduation, I don't have the money—again—to leave town. Savings account now reads, right on schedule, zero—bageled that too. I stay on a year, adjuncting on two campuses, teaching dance, waiting for the next job-search cycle to come around. September, list comes out; October, applications in; November, invitations to interview at professional conference; day after Christmas, go to conference; January, invitations to interview on campus; February, interviews; March, offers come out; July, move to new town; August, start at new school; September, 19th nervous breakdown. *OR,* March, rejection letters pile up; April, 19th nervous breakdown.

I pick up a three-year visiting gig in Idaho—4-4 teaching load, no service required, living-wage salary with benefits. Teach my last dance class and hit the road in a Penske rental van, loaded by roadhouse buddies, towing my pickup, hitched up by roadhouse buddies.

I'll never hear from them again.

———

Pedagogy is a required class in grad school, and I learn about student-centered teaching methods even as I'm teaching dance as a fascist, tyrannical dictator. "Left foot first." Teaching of this sort depends entirely on the teacher's capacity for breaking movement down into its smallest components, and articulating it three ways, in three dimensions, for the three or four different kinds of listeners on the dance floor.

Yes, *listeners*. Not viewers. When a step turns out to be extra-hard for my class, I have them turn their backs to me and *listen*.

They get it instantly.

I have deposited into their brain the best way to think about the action.

Thus I betray my hero, Paulo Freire, the Brazilian educator who, by refusing to deposit knowledge, encouraged students to mount a revolution even as they practiced reading and writing.

I think hard about my training as a vocalist. "Miss Fleisher! . . . Thank you! Not that way! Here's how to structure that measure . . ."

I think about the ballet classes I've seen, how offensive I found it when the teacher, whose graduates comprise ten percent of the New York City Ballet corps, grabbed a student's arm and shoved it into place. How she grasped a student's thigh and twisted it. How she lectured a girl about her weight, till the tutu'd child exited, sobbing.

I'm not exactly humiliating my country-dance enthusiasts, but I am telling them, "Don't just push your hips around in cha-cha. Let the step start on the inside of your foot and roll your foot *out*. Your hips will follow naturally. Think about it. Inside. Out. Inside. Out. Concentrate."

———

My mother and I suffer little "breakups," or so I call them. We become close by letters, then closer, then closer over the phone from thousand-mile distances—then maybe I fly down and visit, sleeping on the porch because she has two cats now—then suddenly something pisses her off and that's it, she's not speaking to me, I die again. Six months later I get a letter about what's going on in her life, as if nothing happened.

Like some wildly wrong wrong wrong couple we start up again, letters, letters, longer letters, phone, maybe a visit.

And again I die.

To live again.

Why don't I break the fuck up with *her*?

For instance, my mother ruins my first wedding. I won't bore you with the details, but here's me at the wedding rehearsal, clapping my hands: "OK, people, listen up—anybody got any questions? Last chance to ask any."

My mother stares at me from across the room. I'm producing this wedding just as I produce my ballets. I'm a born organizer.

"OK, then. Dinner!"

I'm just like her.

I have a lot to learn.

Day of the wedding, friends at the reception approach me gingerly, ask if I have any family there. I point to the toasted bitch in the back corner. She's been downing highballs and talking trash to my new mother-in-law, another drinker. *Her* poison is gin.

"She's pretty," someone says to me.

"Yeah," I say. "I've heard."

When my husband (poor bastard) and I return from a honeymoon (rather lame, hiking around Lake George in the Adirondacks), my mother has left her gift for us on the table by the front door.

It's an envelope. A card.

Shredded. Wee-teeny pieces.

Really teeny—it would've taken extensive effort to tear them that small—I know because it takes a lot of effort for me to put it together, a jigsaw puzzle of the most challenging sort, just to find out how much the bitch had given us in the check that was now a pile of feathers.

A hundred bucks.

A hundred bucks.

Her first child gets married (OK, it's the first of what will be two marriages, but still)—her *only* child, now that the other is pretend-dead—gets married—and her gift is a hundred bucks.

Even adjusting for inflation—that should have been the end for me.

I gather the confetti, place it in an envelope, seal it, and stick it to the bulletin board above my desk.

Whatever I'm going to be, I'm going to be *not this*.

She doesn't speak to me for six months. Then letters. Etc.

When I divorce the poor bastard five years later, while finishing my master's thesis, living in a pressure cooker, she writes me a letter telling me that I allowed my writing ambitions to destroy my marriage.

I wonder if Hemingway's mother ever said that to him.

My mother has not seen either my husband or me since the wedding. My husband and I each have drinking problems I have not succeeded in fixing. I have not discussed this with her, since to do so would be to implicate her own drinking.

She doesn't speak to me for six months. Then letters.

———

Kassie—for so her teachers and schoolmates call her—helps her mother staple and collate materials for her mother's high school English classes. I watch my mother become president of the teacher's union, learn early how to take good messages, reheat pot roast, get softener in the wash. I go to school-board meetings and see my mother at the microphone. I know my mother is nervous but I know I am the only one who knows. When my mother is nervous her ass quivers. I know this from when she has solos in her choral group. Her voice shakes too, but her ass quivers. No one knows to look for this but me. My mother's ass quivers but *still* she takes hundreds of teachers out on strike. My mother is *feel the fear and do it anyway* wonderful.

My brother and I share a common wall between our bedrooms. Down close to the floor, a heating duct opens into both rooms. On Saturday mornings, when there is no school, our mother, exhausted by rage, sleeps until ten. Her children are up much earlier but if we make a sound . . . To get the other's attention, one of us will strum the slats in the vent like we strum my guitar. We whisper and giggle into the vent and then I tiptoe to his room. My brother kicks my ass at Risk—he is always five moves ahead of me and plus, I don't like the game—it's so *guy*—and don't care to give him a good match. I prefer to read. He doesn't like to read unless it's a book about ships. He builds models. For the nine-hundredth time he recites encyclopedic statistics—*with a stutter*—about the USS Iowa until I'm blue with boredom. For the nine-hundredth time I go back to my room and read *Little Women*.

I'm Jo, in love with the German professor.

Our father comprehends none of our erratic behavior.

———

I phone my mother one day when I am thirty-six, and I don't know how, but I can tell it's the end, not just another break-up. "Disowns" is not the right word, since our family owns nothing. On April Fools' Day, no joke. I phone her. *You're a snob, you're an iconoclast, what do you mean "what do I mean," you're supposed to be so smart, look it up, "iconoclast," it means you make fun of me, you try to be better than me, you'll never be happy, we thought you'd be happy when you got a man. Why don't you get a job you* like. *You're not making a living as a writer, you never will—it may be a drag, but there it is. Get over it already. Do you think you're* special *or something?*

"What do you want from me?" *Nothing.*

My mother wanted to be a field biologist. She never wanted to be a teacher, but it was the only professional education available to her. She majored in biology and minored in English.

For reasons she never told me she ended up teaching English instead of biology, and didn't like it very much.

Boys: science, social sciences. Girls: grammar enforcement.

Though she loves to read. As a kid, I watch her consume three one-dollar-paperbacks a week, picked out every Friday afternoon at the bookstore downtown we love to browse in. She calls me over to the tall, metal bookracks that spin the paperbacks around for viewing, holds out a fat Avon with a colorful cover, and asks, "Did I read this one before?" I nod or shake my head, as warranted. My mother's tastes vary widely: Kathleen Woodiwiss, Danielle Steele, Herman Wouk, Irving Stone, Alan Drury; but also, Herman Hesse, *The Rise and Fall of the Third Reich.* By the time I'm fourteen, with my TV viewing limited, I'm reading almost every book my mother brings home (except the *Reich*). The woman chomps through them like popcorn, sitting on one end of the couch every evening with her legs curled under her, smoking cigarettes, gnawing her lip, cracking her chewing gum, getting up only to open a can of beer—the first at nine, second at nine-thirty—all drinking tightly scheduled—third at ten—medicinal—in her case, to treat insomnia.

———

I look at my nails. My mother keeps her nails long and paints them twice a week. So do I.

Although acetone, turns out, fucks up the ozone layer. So I quit.

A glass is picked up and put back down.

Nothing.

I walk downstairs and into the kitchen. My mother sits at the kitchen table with the story in front of her, smoke curling, the fingers of one hand around a can of Carling Black Label.

She is crying, her head low, her other hand holding her forehead.

"How did you know?"

How can we call it *knowledge*? How did it become clear that what happened between my mother and my brother is that my brother finally hit her back? Or that my grandfather hit my mother's mother, and probably my mother as well? No one told me. To this day no one has ever told me. And my grandfather wouldn't hurt a fly, but he hurt *her*. No one *had* to tell me he hurt *her*. I'm the bottom ten percent of my class. Dumb Bunny, dumb bunny, silly wabbit, wabid wabid wodent. In some way or another, all of these people are in love, in twos and threes at sixes and sevens. What do we call it when the obvious, that which requires no evidence, no college degree, no—what do we mean by this—*sense*, of the common or horse varieties—what do we call it when what is clear is hidden in plain sight? Tucked deep in the heave of impenetrable hills, right there for anyone who's willing to get out and walk? Up? And then becomes, as browngreen creek water becomes simply browngreen lake water, clear? How can we call it knowledge when it's a work of *imagining* that informs us?

My mother looks away and sips her beer.

"Not bad," she murmurs finally into the dimness of the dining room. "Not bad."

Tiers

1.

Imagine a classroom in Idaho *third-tier*. Fifty white students circle a room too small for a ring of that size. Five black men sit in the front. A dreadlocked and African-robed administrator leans comfortably against the desk at the base of the chalkboard.

The teacher sits in the back of the room, squeezed in with the white students, taking notes.

At some point Marcus, the university's Diversity Coordinator *all names in this book have been changed, including some place names* finishes his recitation of the programs his office supports, and turns the discussion over to one of the black students, Jesse.

The young man starts in with his usual rant. Testifying, witnessing, *we need more than tales, don't we?* teasing the edges of a titillating truth. His memories, his experiences. His outrage.

Around the room *don't we?* it's the usual. The white women listen alertly, their faces carefully empty. A bit intimidated.

The white men nod their heads robustly, smile broadly, intimidated but refusing to look it. They affirm the stories they hear. When Jesse jokes hintingly about this or that guy he may have roughed up back in the hood—"you know what I'm sayin'?"—they nod harder. I know that it's really Jesse's masculinity they want, Jesse's muscles and hard edges, and that Jesse's hints are designed, probably not consciously, to exploit a cultural bias that indulges male violence. It's Jesse's only means to power: make the white guys envy his supposed capacity for kicking the shit out of them.

So this racialized relation is actually gendered—or, this gendered relation is actually racialized.

But I'm tired. I'm tired of the same talk, going nowhere. And I'm *tired* tired. All the conflict I've faced on this job, all the hatred I've encountered from students, the fear I confront in colleagues. I don't sleep well. It's my third and last semester here, at a university in Idaho that offered me a full-time adjunct gig (subordinate, temporary attachment). The job is contracted to last three years. It pays just enough to live in a tiny city. That is, if you don't meet another English prof online, hook up, and start jetting across the country every fucking month.

"I know what you're saying, bro," one of the white guys says, grinning hard. "I totally hear you, bro."

BRO!

Jesse grins back.

Marcus sits watching, his arms crossed over his chest.

Am I going to do it? Am I going to say it?

I can hardly breathe. Shaking.

One of them—a student I like, who likes me, who is taking his second class with me (this happens to me a lot here)—one of them raises his hand. Jesse calls on him as if he were born to hold the very center of a stage I purposefully, pedagogically (but also personally) shy *shy* away from.

"I want to say that I understand you. We're all the same in here. We all get what you're saying. I want to ask whether you think, though, that you had a right to break the law—I mean, I respect *you*, but I might not always respect what you *do*—and I *do* understand you, bro, I do, but I'm trying to ask whether—"

MY FIST POUNDS MY DESK.

The fingers of that fist joggle loose—notched leaves, on a limb, in a squall.

"*You DON'T understand him, BRO!*" I shout. My voice shakes. "We are *not* all the same! We are *different*! We see things *differently*! Why is it so *impossible* for us to just sit here and acknowledge that my experiences are different from yours? What would be the huge incredible *problem* with that? What is so *threatening* about saying I am what I am and what I am is different from what you are?

"*YOU'RE LISTENING TOO PASSIVELY TO BE ABLE TO UNDERSTAND HIM!*" I bellow. "*YOU'RE NOT HEARING YOUR OWN RESPONSIBILITY IN THIS!*"

The silence is staggering.

I sit and breathe.

Shake.

"And you know what else?" *For some reason I'm not finished yet.* *Joggle.* "If you don't respect what a person *does*, you probably don't respect *them*. Since *when* are we *not* what we *do*?"

Across the room, the student who spoke, a boyish man I've

known for quite some time now, who tells me stories about his wife and the kids they are trying to have at this incredibly young and yet not-so-young Mormon age, slouches pinkly at his desk.

None of the students will meet my eyes.

Jesse stares at me. I can see he is thinking hard.

Marcus uncrosses his arms and sits forward in his desk. "Kassie's right," he says. He looks at the student who spoke. "You're right too. You mean to say that all humans have a great deal in common. That's true. But Kassie is saying that because of the way things tend to go in society, we have some differences among us, and it's important to recognize those and not pretend they aren't there."

I consider flying across the room to kiss him, but I can't even walk. I'm trembling too fiercely.

"That's right," Jesse says, still staring at me. "I appreciate everyone saying they get me, but I'm just trying to show what I know about my life that you don't know about. And there's plenty you don't know."

He's off again. *The stories. What good do the stories do us if we want nothing of them. If we just nod inertly.*

When class is over, the students shuffle out without talking to me. Without even looking at me. They keep a wide, wide berth.

When Jesse leaves he takes a long gaze at me and swings his head. Then he goes.

Marcus meets me in the hall. I'm afraid to look at him but muster up my professional self. "Thanks for getting things back on track," I say.

"I guess it's my opinion," he says carefully, "that losing your temper probably isn't the most effective way of getting things done. You might want to be careful with that."

"Could be," I say.

—— ——

Marcus calls—tiny bit of a crush on him, made a few passes to which he never responded and now it's too late, I just got married—and says we have to get together before I leave town. We've gone a few times to a Chinese restaurant at the bottom of my hill, where the orange chicken is sweet, sticky, and spicy, and we agree to meet there.

Marcus is forever burdened with strays, most of them large men who drop by and stay for a week, eating his food and keeping him up all night with their troubles. Before I leave to meet him he calls again and says, "I have a friend in town. And Jesse wants to come too."

I'm sitting at a booth along the wall, about halfway across the room, when the three men walk in. I'm not expecting to see what I saw, and therefore feel certain *I know I'm right* in thinking that I see the small-built, older man who runs the place bolt a sharp step back when he turns to find the men in front of him. *Understand: he's Asian.* He holds up a finger—"One minute!"—almost defensively, and goes into the kitchen. The men stand there.

All three exchange a glance.

I've been watching the door for almost fifteen minutes—Marcus never was on time—and no one else has been made to wait. Tables are open everywhere.

I wave and they finally see me.

They start toward my table. Jesse leads.

The owner comes out of the kitchen just as they pass its door. He steps forward, blocking their path with his miniscule frame.

Jesse points irritably at me, and I wave and smile as wide as my lips can stretch.

The owner stares.

The four settle in, Jesse next to me.

The new friend, Darryl, used to play football here with Jesse, but he transferred to BYU.

I look at him. "BYU?" I ask. "You transferred to *BYU*?"

"Fucker converted to Mormonism," Jesse says. "He's a fucking *Saint* now. You believe that shit?"

Poor Darryl smiles all through the razzing. He's heard it all a million times, I can tell. "How do you like BYU?" I ask.

He shrugs. "It's ah-ight, I guess."

"Any problems there?"

He looks at Jesse, looks down. "Nah," he says.

Jesse says, "He got him one of them white girls. Found him one of them white college girls in one of them pretty lace dresses with the white stockins."

"Yeah, Jess," I bark, "I know a college girl would be too damn old for you."

He laughs.

"You got a fucking problem with women, Jess," I say. "You're gonna have to work that out some day real fucking soon, OK?"

"I got no problem with women," Jesse says. "I *love* women."

"Right," Marcus says. "You have no problems with women *in general*. Only the ones that land you in *court*."

"I got no problem with her!" He points at me. "She's the coolest of the cool! She be *down!*"

"Bullshit," I say flatly.

He stares at me.

I've been rehearsing this for a month.

"You know I'm racist, right Jesse?"

Marcus sits back in his seat, eyes low.

"I'm racist," I say again.

"Bullshit," Jesse says.

He's looking at me like I just turned emerald.

"I'm anti-racist, but I'm a racist just like anyone else. You know that woman on *Oprah* who says that when she sees a black man on the street she pulls her purse in tighter? I did the same thing this summer in Chicago."

"Get the fuck out."

"I wouldn't shit you. Actually, I think it has more to do with class and gender than race, because I tense up around any man I see on the street who isn't wearing a suit, especially big guys. But anyway, it's true. I mean, I move to the south side of Chicago and all I hear is, Walk here, don't walk there, don't be out past dark, keep your eyes open, watch your back. Do you think my neighbors are advising me to fear *white* guys?"

"So you'd be afraid of me if you saw me on the street?"

I nod.

Jesse sits back and stares at Darryl. "You believe this shit?"

"I'm not an angel, Jess. I'm working at it too." Jesse is shaking his head. "What you need to do is work as hard at gender stuff as I work at race stuff."

"Man. Unbelievable."

We eat.

I've noticed that people are doing double-takes when they pass the booth. It's starting to make me nervous. I feel suddenly unsafe in this white, crime-free, Rocky Mountain paradise.

White woman with three black men. What was I thinking.

Not everyone is safe in small cities that boast of no violence *the odd bicycle theft, the single aggravated assault per day—and these by white men who live in the wrong neighborhoods and anaesthetize themselves with booze and fists and then too the occasional native gone off the rez.*

That's when it happens.

Marcus is talking about something—who remembers what—when Jesse's abrupt bellow cuts him off.

"What are you looking at?" he shouts across the restaurant.

I look where he's looking. An elderly man sits facing us, staring.

"Nothing," the man says quietly.

"Bullshit, 'nothin,'" Jesse yells. "You looking at *somethin* over here!"

"Jesse!" I say.

"Yo," Marcus barks. "Let it go."

"No, I ain't gonna let it go," Jesse shouts. "Every time I look over there all damn night that guy is eyeballing me. You got a problem with me?"

The man shakes his head.

Across the room, the man who runs the place stands watching it all, paralyzed. A young woman *Asian* sits behind the register. Her hand stretches discreetly and settles on the telephone.

"Because I can *give* you a problem with me if that's what you're lookin' for."

"Jesse," Marcus snaps, "chill. He's an old guy, Jesse. Let him go."

"I'll let *him* go if he lets *me* go."

The man's head is practically in his lo mein. The top of his bald head shines right at us.

"He's letting you go. Now just let it be."

"Ah-ight then," Jesse says. "Let's just eat this greasy shit and never come back here again."

"You got a temper on you, Jesse," Marcus says. "You better learn to handle it."

"Yeah well," Darryl says lazily, "it's a heck of a lot better than it used to be."

Jesse laughs.

When dinner's over, we all throw money on the table and Marcus and I, without saying anything, make sure there's an extra-huge tip.

We stand outside in the parking lot.

Jesse points at Darryl. "So if you saw him on the street, you'd be afraid of him?"

I look at Darryl. He's a large man, almost as big as my student Germaine, but more muscular—tight end rather than lineman. He wears a thick gold chain, a polo shirt, creased slacks, and a blazer. He has a wide, sweet-handsome face and a warm grin as he looks back at me looking at him.

I know he knows what I'm going to say.

I smile right at him.

"Hell yeah," I say.

"Damn," Jesse says. "I never heard of such a thing." When he gets into Marcus's car he's still shaking his head.

Darryl climbs in, nodding formally.

Marcus stands looking at me from his car door.

"See ya, Kass," he says.

"See ya, Marcus."

I watch them go.

———

The week I'm leaving, I attend—just for spite—my last department faculty meeting. The program committee chairwoman—my closest friend there, rumored to be my lesbian lover—reports that the race-counseling workshop that made front-page news this week, not to mention TV news coverage, was a wildly successful event that had been organized by *English students!* "These students are to be congratulated," she says proudly. "They're an inspiration to us all."

The name of said students' instructor goes unmentioned—by my closest friend.

The refusal of this committee to fund said successful event goes unmentioned—closest friend.

I look around the room. Everyone nods approvingly, enthusiastically.

Proudly.

No one looks at me.

After I'm gone, word around school is that I left because I wanted to be with my new husband, and that I wanted to write a book.

So I could get a permanent job.

———

December. Two weeks before I leave. Lee Mun Wah's *The Color of Fear* devastates. It makes limp. It makes lump. The workshop is difficult. We are asked to find someone in the audience who is unlike us, and to talk. Mun Wah *actual name: Google him* asks people to come forward and talk about things that have happened to us. To tell our stories. Listeners are asked to respond to what we've heard.

Two hundred people attend. So does a local TV news reporter.

There is a lot of rage, a lot of tears.

I'm so exhausted by my tenuous, repeatedly threatened job situation that when Mun Wah asks how many people feel we've lost jobs because of racism, I overreact and stand up.

I'm the only white person standing.

"These are the heroes, ladies and gentlemen," Mun Wah says.

It's too late to sit down—well, without looking like an asshole.

Part of me is relieved to get these issues out, to be able to sit and talk *finally* about what's going on around us.

A student comes up to me afterward, tears streaming down her face, and gets me in a clutch. "This is the best day of my life," she says.

Part of me is sorrowfully, regretfully wondering how long the chummy high, the warming hugs, the reassurances that result from the workshop will last.

Whether it will change anything.

The student, my student, who organized this event, who raised the money to bring Lee to campus, is higher than high. "Marcus gave me a kiss and said he thought it was an incredible success. He thanked me! So did Jesse!"

"You know," I tell her, "we gotta think about this thing where our codependent tendencies get mixed up with our social concerns and we put all our time into saving people we don't even know very well while we pay no attention to our own lives."

"Right, right, whatever," she says, "but this is *great*, isn't it?"

———

The night before Lee is scheduled to give his four-hour workshop, we take him to dinner. Megan, the organizer, and Marcus and Jesse are there, along with Gary, head of the Gay and Lesbian Association (GALA).

Also in attendance are two white seniors I don't know—a married couple—who serve on the student government committee that eventually, after a great deal of squabbling, put up half the cost of the visit. The Black Student Alliance put up the rest, with contributions from GALA, since I'm their advisor, and the Diversity Committee.

The student government committee is picking up dinner.

The husband is seated at the head of the large table, his wife at his elbow.

Mun Wah is a small, quiet man who listens intently. Gary talks to him about what it's like to be a gay activist on this campus. Megan lists the impossible number of people who turned down requests for the money to bring him in, the number of times they were told that there is no race problem on this campus, the number of times they were told that OK, maybe there is a race problem, but it was up to someone else to do something about it. Jesse tells the story of how the community reacted when he was charged with rape.

The couple fidgets. "We were very glad to help fund this workshop," the husband says importantly, and the wife nods as if this is some profound, personal sacrifice of theirs. "We do think it's important to help race relations. We just hope it can be done in a way that won't upset people."

They're bugging me already—me and my anti-Mormon prejudice. "Why are you concerned with upsetting people?" I ask.

"Well," the wife begins, "it's the students' fee money that supports this event—"

"—the *students'* money," the husband interrupts, folding his hands at chin level in a prayerful, patriarchal gesture, "the *students'* money should be used in ways that benefit the *majority* of students. A discussion of race relations is one thing, but an attack on the values held by the majority of students—this would be a problem."

The wife nods.

It's not my habit to make scenes at dinner *well, and not in the classroom either.* "Isn't that a bit majoritarian of us?" I say nicely.

"Doesn't the majority have some obligation to the minority?" Megan asks. She too is quite nice.

"Don't you *want* to hear about the lives of *minority* students?" Jesse says irritably. He has no qualms about scenes at dinner, I realize. "We pay fees here too. I think the majority of students would benefit from a chance to hear about where some of us come from."

And he's off. Tales of his neighborhood, stories of his attempts to keep his younger brother at the books and out of gangs, eulogies for friends now lost.

Eventually the couple pays the bill and leaves. They do not attend the workshop.

While Jesse is in the men's room, Megan leans over and whispers, "Funny, isn't it, how Jesse is suddenly so enthusiastic about this project?"

I nod.

"And Marcus just now decides it's pretty darn important too," she says. She frowns.

When Jesse returns, Mun Wah addresses him directly. "Jesse," he says in his quiet and heedful voice, "you're very brave to speak up so often in what is obviously a difficult atmosphere. When I told my friends I was coming to Idaho to do this workshop, some of them told me not to come. They were worried that something would happen to me here—they thought I might actually be hurt in some way. So I think you are brave, and you should continue to speak up for your own sake as well as for others."

Jesse listens intently.

"But I'm going to give you some advice about how you're going about it. Stories are good. It's important for us to tell the stories of our lives. But there are times when stories do little more than perpetuate the very stereotypes we are working to undo. Sometimes it's better to employ some analytical strategies to help people understand your perspective. You should work in your education on developing the analytical skills that will help you to provide a more effective argument on your own behalf."

Jesse nods. "Ah-ight," he says. "I hear ya."

———

November. I submit my resignation to the new chair. I've agonized, alone and with Joe—new husband—for two months about the right thing to do. Together we'd made a "decision" that summer. I would break the second of my year-long contracts and resign in December. But I don't really want to. For one thing, I don't like the thought of doing the wonted woman thing, surrendering my job to a man. But it seems brainless to gamble my personal life, health, and writing for a job as untenable as this one has been.

I keep hoping there will be a reason, a way, to stay.

I go to the new chair's office.

I don't know him well. I say, "I'm sorry, I have something I need to talk to you about." And burst into tears.

Oops.

"Oh!" he says, startled. "Are you upset?"

"I think I have to resign my position," I say. "It's been very difficult for me here, and I need time to write a book to get a tenure-track job, and I would like to live with my husband."

"I had no idea it's been difficult for you here," he says. "I'm sorry to hear about it."

How is it possible that he hasn't heard?

"It's a constant struggle," I say, "a constant terror that I'm going to lose my job, a constant fight with the students. Some of them are great, but I have a hard time with how some of them hate me. I need more support than I'm getting."

I say this with rising intonation at the end, as if it were a question.

That is, I want him to provide support, to talk me out of it.

"Well," he says, "I'll have trouble replacing you in mid-year—but I guess that's not your problem. If you feel you need to go, then you need to go."

I stand uncertainly before him, wadding a tissue in my fists.

I submit a letter formalizing the resignation.

Joe on the phone: "You're better off without that fucking place. You did the right thing. We need to be together. You need to write a fucking book so you can get a decent fucking job. We want to have kids."

"So, do ya think he'll call me up later and beg me to come back, like they did with my male colleague, whose resignation they refused to accept? Huh? Huh? Do ya?"

———

November, five weeks before the Mun Wah workshop. My Introduction to Literature class, while reading *Normal Heart*, Larry Kramer's play about the gay men who founded ACT-UP when the AIDS epidemic broke out, giggle about gay male sexuality, but soberly discuss social activism and how it works.

When I show the film *Desert Hearts*, which I choose for its very brief, incredibly mild, and annoyingly romanticized love scene, a quarter of the class gets up in a furor and walks out of the screening. All of them are women.

In my office the next day: a young woman in tears. "Mrs. Fleisher," she says *Mrs. Fleisher she calls me*, "I have plenty of gay friends. I don't have any problem with them as people—I just don't like what they *do*. I *swear* to you that I would have been *just* as upset by having to watch the portrayal of *any* kind of sex."

I try to listen. "The truth remains," I say evenly to the student, "that when I showed *Thelma and Louise* earlier in the semester, no one objected at all—not even the rape scene in that film caused you to walk out of class or to come into this office."

"I didn't like it," she insists. "I just didn't know what to say then."

I had intended to provoke a discussion of the film's failures, its unrealistic depiction of lesbian love, its decision to set these lovers in the unreal time of the fifties, against the mythical backdrop of Reno. I had hoped to talk about how western landscapes like ours in Idaho are used in *Thelma and Louise* and *Desert Hearts* as dreamscapes, liberation-scapes, fantasy power-scapes that perpetuate masculine concepts of the West and say little about the actual, trapped landscapes of most real-life women—they do nothing to propose some new, girl-friendly motif of escape and liberation.

The class never gets there. Instead, we dither and dally over whether this is graphic "filth." The film didn't bother most of the men, so we talk about two-women pornography in our culture—most of the men claim never to have seen any, but clearly it's made its way into their social consciousness—and how this sort of pornography reinforces the masculine power structure.

As Berger might say, women are all about the male gaze. No gaze, no woman.

One of the men generously admits that if it had been two men making love, he might have freaked too. Seeing the actual images in *Desert Hearts* is more shocking than the pictures his imagination produces in reading *Normal Heart*.

A group of students go to the dean to complain about me and ask that I be fired. As usual, the students themselves don't tell me they have done this, but it gets back to me via the classmates to whom they boast. I lose more sleep, wait for the dean to call, for my job to be threatened once again. The dean knows me—me, temporary, subordinate—through my work on the university-wide Diversity Committee—in fact, I may be the only adjunct faculty member in English he does know.

He never calls.

He never called.

Third semester. A student, Hannah, has disappeared from class. Her husband Curt misses a class and then comes back looking a little haggard. He comes up to me after class.

"Hannah lost a baby," he says. "So she won't be here for a while."

"Oh shit," I say. "She was pregnant?"

"About nine weeks. We just found out a month ago."

"Is she OK?"

He shakes his head. "She lost a lot of blood. She's out of the hospital, though. Doing better."

"Are *you* OK?"

He's trying to laugh. He shakes his head again. "It was rough."

"Do you have any family around here? Anyone to help take care of her?"

"Her family kind of has a problem with me, so they don't come around much. And my family, my family's cool, but they're down in Atlanta. They've never even been up here. I think they're afraid of getting shot or something." He tries to laugh again.

"Well, you tell her we're all thinking of her."

"Look," he says, "I'd like to tell the class but there's some folks in here who just aren't cool, you know? So can we just say she's not feeling well? And I'll tell the people who *are* cool."

Curt keeps coming to class and Hannah finally shows up when we all go out to breakfast to celebrate the end of the semester. She entertains them with funny stories about what it's like being married to a black guy in Idaho.

"When we met at school," Curt says, "it was like, Wow, someone who gets it."

"The good news is he wants to be a doctor," Hannah jokes. "I keep telling my mother, You *told* me to marry a *doctor*! I always do what I'm *told*!"

It's around then that Germaine goes missing. He comes to class one day, his eyes red. "I gotta leave town," he tells me, his head hanging again.

"What's up?"

"Trouble at home. I gotta get back there."

"What is it?"

"My best homeboy went down." He's staring at his shifting feet.

"Excuse me?"

"My buddy. Got killed. Got shot. Fucking Crips took him out."

"Gangs?"

"Yeah. Fucking assholes, man. I gotta go home and do something about it."

"Is there a funeral?"

"Yeah."

"You coming back?"

He lifts his head and stares off in the distance.

"Yeah."

"I'm so sorry about your friend."

"I gotta leave town."

"You come back. We'll work it out."

He nods, and is gone.

He does come back. But he cuts classes left and right, and the unfinished and late papers I'm accustomed to receiving become no papers at all. I talk to Jesse. "Man, I been trying to get him to get his shit together. He says he don't have no more money, and I tell him to come over and we'll feed him. But he just won't come around no more. I heard he had it out with the coach and quit the team, but he won't even answer his goddamn pager."

"He looked pretty freaked when his friend got killed."

"It's a bad scene, man. He's gonna end up back in it, way he's headed."

Jesse and Curt keep the class focused on race till some of the white students are sick of it.

"I just don't know what we're achieving here," Rob says one day. He's taken to cutting classes too. "I'm not a racist. I'm trying to get an education so I can get a *job*, not to talk about *this* stuff every day. If bad things have been done to these people, it wasn't me."

"Where'd you get the idea that education is about getting a job?" I say.

"What you mean, you're not a racist?" Jesse says, ignoring me. "Everyone's a racist."

"It's just not true," a woman pipes up. "Maybe we all have prejudices, but we're not all racists."

"Problem is," Curt says, "it's embedded so deep in the system that it takes a whole semester to root it out so we can even look at it. And by the time it's dug out for analysis, we're tired of it already."

"Right," I say. "What else is the study of writing and literature about, but the analysis of interpretations that differ?"

"*What's* rooted in the system?" Rob barks *ignored again.* "Listen, I went to China to witness to people. Those people are people of color too, and I went there not because I was racist but because I cared about them enough that I wanted to bring them the word."

"Whoa, whoa," Curt says. "You're not racist, but you go there to save their souls. What about *their* religion? Don't you have any respect for *their* religion? What's the matter with Buddhism? Why don't you leave them alone?"

It's threatening to boil over into a brawl. "Hold up for just a second," I say. "Let's just take a breath. Where do the rules for most religions come from?"

"The Bible," someone says.

"Or some other sacred book," a Mormon student corrects.

"OK. Let's look at the Book of Mormon, then," I say. "What's up with the thing about the Lamanites?"

No one answers. They all look puzzled.

"In the Book of Mormon," I say, "the Lamanites are people whose skin was turned dark to punish them for being bad people and to make sure they wouldn't mix with the good white people. If they're good, in heaven their skin turns white again. What's up with that?"

Jesse slams his hand on his desk. "Yeah," he says, "what in the hell is up with *that*?" Curt shakes his head.

The Mormon students are still looking puzzled. "I don't believe you," Rob says. "I've never heard such a thing. Not from the Saints."

I shrug my shoulders. "It's there," I say. *Yeah. I actually read parts of it. And it's every bit as badly written as they say.*

"I've never heard that either," a woman says. "If it's in there, the Saints obviously aren't preaching it anymore, so it isn't relevant anymore. It shouldn't have any impact."

Jesse sighs loudly. Curt's still shaking his head. "So if it's in the book," I say, "but it isn't being preached anymore, it's OK? It has no effect on what we do today? We can ignore it?"

"Of course we can't ignore it," Curt says. "Those books define who we are. They tell us where we came from. How can we go anywhere new if we keep pretending these things don't exist?"

See also I Timothy 2:11-12.

"This is not to pick on the LDS," I say. "Right? We could just as easily look at the Catholic church. What did you think about that article we read about how the Pope condoned slavery by agreeing—due to economic pressures—that dark-skinned people were savage? And you know I'm an atheist"—I yank my eyes to the crap institutional carpet to avoid their discomfort with that—"but my family's church, the Methodist church—we waged a campaign in the western United States in the nineteenth century to take native kids away from their parents, put them in boarding schools, and beat the Indian out of them. Education as cultural assimilation. How am I supposed to move forward if I decide to forget my church did that?"

"But the Lamanites," Rob says, "from what *you* say about them anyway—that's nothing as bad as slavery or kidnapping Indians. That's just a *story*. The Saints have never actually *done* anything like that."

"The Mormons," Curt says, "were involved in the single largest act of genocide in U.S. history—the Bear River Massacre—and for a while they've been part of keeping that story quiet."

Rob throws up his hands and falls back in his seat. His face is rosy.

"OK," I say *professional referee*, "time out again. Here's the thing. You see history one way, Rob, and Curt sees it another. The question is, what should we do with these conflicting histories? And what is the appropriate response when people tell you, Hey, your people hurt my people? What should we do when that happens? As writers, trying to advocate for our own perspectives, what are our obligations to readers with other perspectives?"

"I think we should listen," a woman says. "We don't necessarily have to agree with someone, but if they're telling us that we did some damage to them, we should at least listen."

"That's what I'm writing my paper about," another woman says. "We tend to sit in here and shout at each other, but at some point we have to actually *do* something. At some point we have to stop shouting and work together to figure out where to go from here."

———

Third-and-last semester. I agree to serve as faculty advisor to the Gay and Lesbian Association, which has gone without an advisor for some time. As adjunct faculty, I have no clout and few contacts with which to help them. But the president of the group, Gary, is a student in one of my classes, and he asks me to do this as a favor. They can't collect their student government appropriation without an advisor.

Immediately, I hear rumors that I'm gay. My lover, it's said, is a female faculty member with whom I lunch weekly—head of the program committee.

No women attend the GALA meetings. I squirm in my seat—the only woman and the only heterosexual. For a while I want to be just about anywhere else.

Among the men present, the fear is palpable. "I'm afraid to come here," one man says. "I could be shot on my way out for all I know."

"I'm concerned about losing my job," says another.

There is some discussion about what the group can do to support a man who's being evicted from his apartment after eight years of living there—the landlord, he's certain, has discovered that his tenant is gay. The "reasons" for the eviction are bullshit, he says.

I look over both shoulders on my way to my car.

Meanwhile, a student in my literature course, as her project for the class, invites a group of lesbians to visit class while we're reading literature by gays, to talk about what their lives are like. The class is mesmerized but I'm skitchy *too much like show and tell.* One woman seems particularly nervous—she talks so softly the class must lean in to hear. She narrates her reluctance to come out to her family, insists that her parents must know that this woman she has lived with for five years is more than a roommate—but she's afraid to force them to confront the obvious. She's in tears as she describes the harrowing homophobic jokes *normalizing humor* her father makes frequently. She talks about her job as a school bus driver, which she likes very much, and which she's certain she'll lose if her private life becomes public. She relates several incidents in which her house has been attacked—bottles thrown, trash dumped.

But, she says, given the anti-gay legislation being proposed again that year in Idaho, she has vowed to speak out about her life.

"You can't do *nothing*," she says. "You can't sit by quietly."

This is her first time speaking in public, to strangers, about how she lives, who she loves *narrative as subversion when it's narration of the unheard, the unwritten.*

I tell my lunch companion that these class visits trouble me. "I feel like I'm running a circus," I say. "Look, kiddies! Look at the blacks! Look at the lesbians! Aren't they *cute?*"

"I wouldn't worry unless they start bringing popcorn," she says.

I finally receive my student evaluations from the semester prior. They've been picked over and held for months by the outgoing chair.

They're even better than those from my first semester, as more and more students hear about what I'm doing and seek out my classes for their own purposes. But students who are in the courses accidentally and who deeply resent my goals are still venomous.

GO BACK TO YOUR RADICAL-INFESTED CITY AND STAY THERE! writes one in huge letters across the comment section on the back.

Me? A "radical"?

Damn. If they ever saw a REAL radical, they'd faint dead in their tracks.

And I hate cities *genetic white fright.*

I tape the comment to my office door.

Two weeks after the lesbians' talk, on trick-or-treat night, the student who organized the women's visit to the class finds that her pickup truck has been tricked-out. Spray-painted.

"Die Lesbo Bitch!" her truck reads, in uneven, black letters that sprawl the entire length of the old, gray Ford.

———

Third-and-last semester *three strikes*. An episode of *Oprah* is what does it.

The show airs early in September. It's a Friday, I'm exhausted, I miss Joe, I'm sick of talking to him on the phone, I'm crashed on the couch with the remote control and plan a nap. Surf channels a bit first.

And there is Lee Mun Wah.

"Today we're not just going to talk about racism. We're going to do something about it."

Says one of the richest women in the world.

I sit straight up and put the remote down.

Mun Wah is based in Los Angeles. An African American man who was trying to rob the family business killed Lee's Korean immigrant mother. Lee gave up a teaching career to make a film called *The Color of Fear*, which he uses to conduct workshops on racism all over the country for government agencies and corporations.

His performance on *Oprah* is electric.

We've got to get this guy here, I think.

But how?

The phone rings.

"Are you watching this?!" It's Nicole, an undergrad *not a student of mine, but still* with whom I'm friendly. "I know how you love this shit," she says. We talk for a while, promise to see each other tomorrow at the yard sale we're doing *got to drain some ballast before moving* with some other friends, and I'm back to watching the show.

The phone rings.

"Turn on *Oprah*!" a student yells into the phone. "This guy is great!"

Megan drives across town early the next morning on her way to her job at ZCMI, the Latter-day-Saints-owned department store, to find me at the yard sale. She makes a beeline from her car.

"You won't believe what I saw last night," she says.

"I do believe it," I say.

"Hey," Nicole yells at Megan, "I'm here too!"

"Oh, hi," Megan says distractedly, and then turns back to me. "We have to get him here."

"I know," I say, "but I can't figure out how."

"We can do it. It's going to be my project for the class."

I require the students to perform one activist project inspired by the literature they're reading.

I shake my head. "He can't be cheap, Megan. I don't think we can raise the money."

"We can do it. We have to be able to do it." She marches back to her car without lifting her eyes from the grass, drives off without waving.

"God," Nicole says. "Now that she's found you she doesn't love *any* of us lowly *students* anymore."

In class on Monday a student bursts in. "Did you see it?" She's waving a video. "I taped it!"

I show the video to all four of my classes. Reactions vary. The usual bored stares from white students who don't want to be confronted with these issues. Wild enthusiasm from students who think a visit from this guy might make a difference. Indifference from students who think that the workshop would just be more talk with no point.

Jesse and his friend Germaine have their doubts.

But when Megan tells the lit class that, as her class project, she's organizing a group to raise the two thousand dollars necessary to bring him to campus, fully a fourth of the class signs on to help. She's already signed the contract and made a date with Lee: December 8.

The last week of classes.

They have less than three months to find the money.

"I don't think it can be done," I tell her, wincing, wishing Megan hadn't signed. "But I admire you for trying."

"Aw, shut up," she says. "If I listened to you I wouldn't even *be* in this class!"

While they continue their studies, along with the usual arguments about how to interpret the expressions of people different from them, the students arrange bake sales, write grant proposals, and stage presentations to various community groups in the hopes of finding some money.

I bake some of my world-famous brownies for the sales and send a proposal to the program committee in my own department. It's turned down flat. My lesbian lover tells me that one committee member insisted that this sort of thing is not what a literature course is supposed to do.

Huh.

Megan calls, frustrated. "I keep asking Marcus for help, and he keeps blowing me off. He's distracted, he says he's busy, he says he'll get back to me and he doesn't. And Jesse won't help either. I'm getting no more help from black men than I'm getting from white men."

"Let's think about this," I say. "We probably look like a couple of bleeding heart liberal white chicks stealing what they think of as their issue, their story. Maybe we get in their way."

"I think they just have no respect for women," she says. "No matter what I do, they're never going to let me in their club. I'd really like to have their respect, and it's not going to happen."

"Might not."

Megan had taken my comp class during my first semester in Idaho. She's a little older than average, and it turns out that we have a mutual friend—Nicole—at the university, and that her husband is distantly related to my best friend from graduate school *the only person who told me not to take this job. HUGE crush on him but that's a story for another day.* Megan's husband is a student of mine too, both of them in composition, but in different sections. She often came to my office to ask how Cameron was doing. "Was his paper OK?"

Megan is a Mormon.

I've had a hard time getting used to this thing where very young, married Mormon couples are in my classes together, with the wives nursing the husbands through, and the husbands cutting the wives off in discussion. The first day of my first class there, a woman—this one not enrolled in the class—walks into the classroom at the end of the meeting and says she's sorry but her husband can't make it to class and she's there to get the syllabus and assignments for him.

I'm stunned. "Your husband can get his *own* syllabus," I bark. "And he needs to speak to me *himself* about having missed the first class. He needs to hear *himself* what he's being asked to commit to in this course."

I have no idea that this is accepted practice in this neck of the high plains desert—which means that I come off as Bitch of the Universe.

Invariably, the wives earn the higher grades.

"You're as bad a codependent as I am," I tell Megan, "and Cameron's paper is his own damn business."

She laughs. "I know," she says, "I can't stop myself."

When the course is over, we become friends. Megan loves to tell me the story of her women's studies professor at a different university. "I thought she was nuts," she says. "And she was doing totally what you're trying to do. I just didn't get her then. But now I see exactly what she was up to. A lot of these students who don't get you now, they'll probably get you later."

"I can't wait," I say. "You should write her a note and tell her this," I say. "She's probably suffering like I am."

We enjoy many lunches together, most of them with our friend Nicole, a returning English major, nearly my age, who's fighting through a divorce. We dish about men and talk about school.

We talk religion. "I'm a Mormon," Megan says, "but not one of these Utah Mormons. That's what my mother calls them. When you grow up in another city, like I did, you don't grow up in a place where Mormons control everything. You see other kinds of people. You know more about other perspectives."

"Fucking Mormons," Nicole says. "They're so sheltered. Everyone has to see things their way."

Megan nods.

"I want to take your lit course," Megan announces one day.

"What the fuck for?" I ask. "You're a junior, you're finished with your requirements, you're a psych major."

"It sounds really interesting. It sounds like exactly the kind of thing I need to open my eyes a bit."

I shake my head. "It's not a good idea," I tell her. "You and I are friends now. That causes a lot of complications." I tell her that the other students will sense our relationship, resent her, and mistrust me.

"I'm sorry," I say. "I would prefer it if you didn't."

"Are you telling me that I can't?"

I don't know what to say. I always try to avoid *dodge* prescriptive directions to students. "I'll leave it up to you," I say, "but I wish you wouldn't, and if you do it, I want you to be aware of the problems it could cause for you. You'll be alienated from your peers."

She enrolls for the following fall.

"Right off the bat you get a fucking *F* in following instructions," I say.

———

Third-and-last semester *again*. The lit class meets right after Jesse's comp class, and Jesse has taken to following me down the hall to the lit class, bringing a bunch of his friends, to sit in and comment. His friend Germaine comes along too, to this same course he took last semester—*alone*. But this time, with reinforcements, he isn't afraid to speak. For a moment, the white students are a bit tense *me too* as this group of black men lines the rear wall of the classroom in a solid, immovable row. The men describe conditions in the ghettoes *their word* and the white students listen raptly, their eyes open wide. Although they have not respected the truths of the literature I have put in front of them, and they do not respect me when I attempt to defend the validity of that literary perspective, they do not fuck with these men.

Jesse testifies. He witnesses. He tells story after story to the class, bringing Germaine and other men into the stories to affirm what he's saying. He alludes amorphously to the life of lucrative crime he led before buckling down, with the help of his mother, to studies and a football scholarship. The students giggle at his hints about drug running and violence. Jesse displays scars from knife fights. "I haven't been an angel, Lord knows that," he says with a grin. "I done some things I ain't proud of. I done them young enough so they didn't really hold me back—but still, I done them. I got a temper on me, I admit. I get into trouble. But I've decided to be done with that, and when I get my degree I'm going back, and I'm going to work to make sure my little brother and as many kids as possible keep theirselves together and get an education like I got."

The white students grin when they hear this. "I hear ya, bro," says a male Mormon student, nodding his head chummily. A lot of the other men nod readily too.

Bro?

Good god.

"I wonder if we can explore the stereotypes we have in this country regarding poverty," I say. "Do me a favor and try this. I'm going to describe a family to you, and you tell me what color it is. OK?"

They nod.

"OK. All told, the current generation of this family has eleven grandkids in it. One of the uncles is currently in prison for assault with a deadly weapon, after a long career of breaking and entering. Two girls got pregnant when they were sixteen and dropped out of high school. They were on welfare for a while and still live with their mother. Two boys got teenaged girls pregnant and had to marry them, but the marriages didn't last and the girls are on and off of welfare depending on what sort of job they can get. Three boys went into the Navy so they'd get straightened out, but one got kicked out for drugs. One girl is 'retarded.' One girl was homeless for a while. One girl went to college.

"OK. What color is that family?"

"Black." Several students say it quietly, almost inaudibly, under their breath.

You know where this is going, I know.

"That family," I say, "is *my* family."

Well. On my mother's side. Solid, rural middle class on my father's side—rural, which means no-real-assets middle class—but I didn't grow up with him.

You can hear the ripples of muffled shock spread across the room. Jesse too.

"If I'd told you that some of them live in trailers, would that have given it away for you?"

They nod.

"These stereotypes regarding poverty and the working classes—where do they come from? Are the different races really all that different at those income levels? Why aren't 'they' part of 'we'?"

I tell Jesse after class, "You know, they treat you like a fucking movie star. They've seen you on TV, you know. They think they're looking at a real live Ice T or some shit. A fucking Tupac."

Jesse grins widely. "Whatever it takes to get them to listen," he says.

I rattle my head. "I don't know about this," I say.

———

Although committee service isn't required for the faculty with three-year, temporary appointments, I've joined the Diversity Committee that first semester, become friends with Marcus, the campus Diversity Coordinator, and connected with people who could send me students of color. My first black student, Germaine, a defensive lineman for the football team, appeared in my second semester, squeaking through my lit class.

Thanks to him, maybe, by my third semester, I finally have a reputation with the Athletic Department. Jesse and Germaine usually come together, and I notice a difference in Germaine's behavior. When he's with Jesse, his head is up, his headphones are down, he listens and laughs.

And Curt. Curt doesn't know Jesse or Germaine. He isn't a football player and resents the fact that everyone who meets him on campus assumes he is. He's pre-med, he likes to lift weights, and he's brilliant, one of the smartest students I've ever had anywhere. Never misses a class, never misses a deadline, reads everything I mention to him and comes back for more, writes insightful, bitingly funny papers about racism in Idaho, and the profound way the anticipation of a racist audience alters his writing and thinking.

I notice that Curt comes to class every day trailing a redhead, Hannah, who walks in just a few seconds behind him, looks furtively about the class and sits down in a chair next to him—but not too close.

It's a much smaller class than the lit class—about fifteen students.
Three out of fifteen.
Much better odds than one out of fifty.
Three over-sized black men make me just a bit uncomfortable.
But also.
Damn near everything I know about my own racism, sexism, heterosexism, etc.—about my white privilege—I've learned from students.

Jesse makes a point of dragging Germaine into the conversation, and Germaine rattles on mumble-quick for whole paragraphs. He looks more confident. But still the papers are late, the books are never there.

The moment of learning is the moment of discomfort. It's the transition between knowings.

Jesse says, "I'm trying to make sure Germaine gets the reading done. He comes over to my place and we give him dinner and man can that boy *eat*! But you know, the coach is riding him, man. Don't know what's up with that, but the coach ain't happy."

I go to a football game just to watch Germaine standing down there by the bench. Jesse is a fifth-year senior who's played out his eligibility, so he's on the sidelines, running between coaches. Germaine gets to play in the fourth quarter, makes a couple of good tackles. The newspaper carries a picture of him crawling off a pile-up that stopped the other team's last-minute drive. In class I tell him I saw the big play, and he breaks into a beaming, blushing grin. "That was really good the way you read that play as going left when everybody else went right," I say.

"You like football?" he asks, looking surprised.

"Not so much as I used to," I say. "You seem to like playing it."

He nods. "But I got problems with this coach all of a sudden. He wants this and that and I just don't want to."

"Maybe Jesse can help," I say, and he nods again.

But. I've heard some rumors. A bunch of football players went to a bar one night after a game and met four town girls *understand: white* apparently under age. The four couples had consensual sex and the players are being charged with statutory rape. Because I'm disgusted with the whole story, I tune out, discard my newspaper, pay no mind.

Jesse hasn't been in class for a week. Germaine showed up the first day Jesse missed but has since vanished along with Jesse.

When Jesse comes back he's wearing a suit. The students stare at him, and he seems to be holding back warily. "What's the occasion?" I say *stupid as ever*. "You gettin' married or somethin'?"

His head drops a bit. "Gotta go to court," he says.

"Everything all right?"

"Will be."

He doesn't speak as much in class as usual—it's clear he hasn't done the reading. Germaine trails into class late and mute.

When I get home the newspaper waits as always on my front step. Under the banner, above the fold, unavoidable, the official player photographs of four young African American men look back at me with tough, reserved grins.

The hall of shame.

And there's Jesse.

"Players Plead No Contest, Lose Scholarships."

The furor goes on for weeks. Jesse insists there was a deal. The coach had said that if they pleaded no contest and accepted 200 hours of community service, they could keep their scholarships. But at the hearing, the judge announced that they would be losing their scholarships, which is not the judge's prerogative and none of his business. Turned out that university officials had pressured the coach into rescinding the scholarships, and the coach hadn't told the players the deal was off before they went to court and pleaded out.

None of this much affects Jesse, who isn't eligible to play anymore anyway, and already has a criminal record. But the other three men will have to leave school.

The Black Student Alliance stages demonstrations to protest the loss of the scholarships, the breaking of the deal. Townspeople *all white* are just as enraged that the four men received no jail time. The fury swells until university administrators are forced to hold a public "information session" in which they explain their actions to both sides.

At which session, one administrator answers black student concerns by asserting that recruiting a winning team may be a good thing, but not if winning means the sacrifice of public safety.

The picture painted is one of two-legged animals imported for the purpose of performing in the coliseum, but escaping their cages and raping womenfolk on their off hours.

Ms. Magazine, my most beloved publication, runs an outdated notice objecting to the first announcement—that the players will not lose their scholarships and will be punished only with community service. That picture is one of young girls being preyed upon by older, stronger men who rape with impunity.

The notice doesn't point out that all the players are black, and all the girls are white, and that the community context is one of racialized, class-specific, religious conflict.

Nor does it ask about the responsibility of the girls, who were in a bar alone after midnight, or about the responsibility of parents whose children troll bars at unreasonable hours.

As it happens, our class is starting the section on gender.

I can't help but razz Jesse some before class. "Like 'em young, huh Jess?"

"No way did I know those girls were fifteen years old," he says.

"Yeah," Germaine says, "they had a shitload of make-up on—I was there, I thought they were twenty, no shit."

"Aw c'mon, twenty's too damn old for young Jesse here," I say, "we all know that."

Jesse grins sheepishly. "Next time I'll ask for I.D.," he cracks.

He isn't particularly interested in extended conversations about gender issues, and pretty much tunes out the next two weeks. I keep challenging him to make connections. "If it's true that slavery was first practiced on women and children when private property came along, and later applied to men of lower classes and men of color, doesn't it make sense to think that racism will never disappear until sexism disappears?"

"But that ain't sexism," he says. "Men are stronger than women, so they have to do different things. Men can't have the babies. We have to divide what we do."

"It's important to support the family," says Rob. "The family is really suffering these days, and both men and women need to remember their roles."

Jesse nods.

"What *are* their roles?" Hannah asks. She's come alive in these discussions of gender issues.

"Men need to be involved with their children," Rob says, "but they also need to work to *support* those children, and women need to do what they do better than men, which is to be home *raising* those children."

Jesse and Rob are now nodding at each other warmly.

Strange bedfellows.

"So if I were doing what I was supposed to," I say, "I wouldn't be here teaching you right now. I'd be with my new husband, raising children."

No answer.

I turn to Jesse. "What if I said to you that based on the color of your skin, you were going to have to give up your dream of becoming a teacher and a coach and stay home and raise kids? What if I told you that people your color are just better at it than people my color, so, I'm sorry, but you'll have to give up being a coach? And it's just *your* tough damn luck for being so damn *good* at it."

"It's not the same thing!" Jesse says.

"Why not?" Curt says.

"Because both black and white people can have babies, but only *women* can have babies. It's not about race, it's about biology."

Hannah has had it with him. "Biology was used to argue that

black people are less intelligent than whites," she snaps. "Hell, it's still used that way sometimes. Isn't that the same thing? You have black skin, so you're stupider than me and you can't go to college? And I have a uterus, so I'm smarter with kids and I can't go to college?"

Jesse shakes his head.

"Sometimes," Curt says, "to see how similar some of these race and gender problems are, you have to be married to someone who's not the same color as you."

———

At the last department meeting of my second semester at Idaho, the chair begins his remarks by saying that he's talked things over with the dean of the college, and he'll be stepping down from his position as chair before his current term is up. His resignation will be effective that summer.

He gives no reason.

The senior women stare straight ahead, expressionless.

———

For my second semester, I manage to get a course approved called The Literature of Revolution. We'll read works by people of color, by women, by working class peoples, by gays and lesbians, and assess the contributions of these literatures to social change. Can literary narrative provoke action?

Germaine is there the first class. He's a huge young man, has to be over 300 pounds—loping, tight-lipped. His head hangs perpetually at the level of his collarbone, and he shuffles slowly down the hall, tuned in to god knows what on his headphones, his eyes working their corners warily.

There are more than fifty students at the first class. In an attempt to avoid an "unacceptable drop rate," I have overenrolled and let in a bunch of my students from last semester, hoping for a big exodus after the first meeting. I've been getting phone calls from students wanting to know exactly what "Literature of Revolution" is, and whether they'll be reading Thomas Jefferson.

Um—no.

Alexis de Tocqueville?

No.

Thomas Paine?

NO.

Germaine grabs the chair closest to the door in the back of the large, over-crowded room.

He's the only person of color there.

I can tell he's freaking a bit when I explain what the course will consist of. His head drops to his desk, and he glances sideways at the other students when they start talking about race relations in Idaho. The other students are hyper-conscious of his presence as well, and seem reluctant to volunteer any opinions about how well the white and black populations get along in town, or how well the whites and nearby Shoshone and Bannock get along.

He cuts the next few classes. But so do a bunch of other students, as predicted.

Then he reappears.

I walk up to him after class and break into my kidding-grin *condescension, literally.* "Where the hell you been?"

The corners of this colossal man's mouth twitch upward as he concentrates on his shoes. "Oh, you know."

"Where's your book?"

"I ain't got it. I been meanin' to get over there, but—you know."

"Germaine," I say. I take his arm, something I don't do with students I don't know well *generally try even then to keep it to a minimum*. I'm tease-smirking when I do it. He's the size of two and a half of me. He looks down at me and smiles back. "I need you to get the book and read it and get to class and talk about what you think."

He nods. "Ah-ight."

I start off the course talking about class issues, and then move to race. We read Tillie Olsen, Countee Cullen, Alice Walker, Amiri Baraka, Booker T. Washington, Richard Wright, W. E. B. DuBois, Toni Cade Bambara, Charles Wadell Chestnutt, Nadine Gordimer *through literature I gain access to a consciousness that is not mine.*

Germaine makes maybe every other class. He never brings a book. He never opens the worn notebook he carries with him each time.

"But this is stupid," one of the white students complains, Alice Walker's book in front of him, shut tight. "Why does her mother make her give back the quilt?"

"Because," another student answers, "she's defining heritage in this thing that belongs to her sister—this quilt—she's turned the idea of a personal heirloom into some piece of art that belongs in an antique store. This African American Heritage thing."

"I don't see that," another student chimes in. "What is this heritage thing? Isn't she just an American? Why do they have to have a heritage that has nothing to do with *us*?"

In the back of the room, Germaine's head elevates a fraction.

"Yeah, what is this stuff with her calling herself by an African name? She's not African."

"And why do they have to identify themselves that way at all? Why don't they identify as just *Americans*? Like the *rest* of us do."

Germaine's head retreats as he fidgets in his seat.

Say something.

When the hour is up, I remind the class of their next reading assignment and give them my food for thought for next time:

"Why is there a we/they thing happening in here? What's up with that? Why are *we* using the word *'they'*? *Is* there a we/they? Or are we more or less the same? How should we address each other?"

Germaine hangs back. He looks strange. He stands in front of my office door and examines his sneakers.

"Wanna talk?" I say to him.

He nods.

He spills into the chair on the other side of my desk while I prop the door open *always keep the door open.* I pull my chair out from behind my desk so there will be nothing between us.

"'S'up?" I say *condescension: the inappropriate appropriation of dialect.*

"It's so hard for me to sit in there," he says, studying the fibers of the office carpet. His vast hands and feet will not be still. He rubs the arms of the chair, crosses and uncrosses his shins.

"What are you thinkin' when you're in there?" I ask.

He shakes his head. "It's just so hard."

When he talks, he speaks with his head down, and fast, and in a muttering torrent that makes him hard to comprehend. I lower my own head by way of picking up what I can.

"They just don't get it," he says, "they don't know nothin' bout where I come from and they talk like the things they know about is the only things that matter anyway and they just don't know *shit* and they read that stuff and they talk that talk and they just don't know *nothin'*. It's hard, it's hard for me to sit in there and listen 'cause you know, man, I come from someplace else and what they don't know 'bout where I come from is *way* more than what I don't know bout where *they* come from, and that ain't fair, you know what I mean? You know what I mean? I mean, they just talk and talk like they know stuff, and it's just really hard for me. It's just really hard. I mean, sometimes I just feel *sick*."

"Germaine," I say, "is that why you're not comin' to class?"

He sits up a little. "Well, you know, I ain't so good about gettin' to class anyway, you know, I gotta lot of problems of my own, you know what I mean? I gotta lot of people countin' on me back home, you know, my folks, the hood. And I got football and alla that, you know what I mean."

"But this doesn't help."

He shakes his head.

"Where's home?"

"L.A."

"*Shit*, you come the whole way up here from L.A.? You must feel like you're in *hell*."

He smiles slyly at my idiotic jive.

"Well, if it makes you feel better, I'm in hell too. This place is fucked up, isn't it?"

For once, he looks right at me and laughs. *Yeah. Women cuss. So do teachers.*

"You doin' the readings?" I say, putting on my bitchy school-marm voice.

"Well, you know, I try, I do what I can, but thing is, I ain't got the money for the book, know what I mean? I mean, I just got problems. But I think I'm gonna have the money together soon."

I pull a complimentary examination copy of the book off my shelf and give it to him. "Here," I say. "A gift from the publisher."

He sits with the heavy book in his huge hands. He rolls it around like it might-could bite him. "Wow," he says. "Thanks."

"Germaine," I say, "can you talk in class? Because the thing is, they just aren't gonna learn anything about you and where you come from unless you tell them. Know what I mean?"

He nods.

"Though the problem of course is that maybe you don't want to be the guy in charge of educatin' the white-folks. Which is OK too."

"Yeah, man, that's definitely where it's at, I mean, they're gonna tell you you're wrong anyway when there ain't no brothers around to back you up, know what I mean? And then I just get in a hassle with them and I don't wanna mess up your class, neither."

"It's not my class," I say. "It's *your* class. But look, it's not all of them, right?"

He shakes his head hard. "No, some of them are really nice, and they talk to me, you know, when we do that small group stuff you got us doing. But them others, man . . . You know who I mean. They just not up for listenin' to nobody. No point, man."

He looks at his watch. "Shit, I'm late for class." He stands up and shuffles his big feet, shifts the headphones around his neck. I stand up too.

"Look, Germaine, I'm going to need papers from you. You write about this if you want. I want to help you in this course, but I gotta ride your ass about the work, too. OK?"

He nods.

"So you get me a paper next week. And try to take a deep breath and talk in class once or twice. Might help keep you from exploding."

"Ah-ight, Doctor Fleisher," he says—he always calls me that, when all the others call me Kassie, or Mrs. Fleisher, even when my syllabus clearly states my name as "Dr. Fleisher" *snob!* He looks relieved. Then he goes.

2.

Imagine your boss is a bishop.

Second semester. The Literature of Revolution course goes so well that I propose it again for the third semester. Several of my composition students want to take it and Marcus says he has plenty of students he could send if it were taught again.

The proposal is rejected. No reason is given. I'm assigned a section of Introduction to Literature.

Bastard.

OK, I think. No problem. There's no rule that says I can't cover the same material in the Intro class. I'll just teach the Literature of Revolution class under the Intro name. I fill out my book order for the following semester with the same works I'm using now.

The Bishop *oops, I mean "department chair"* calls me in. "Just got your book order," he says. He's acting friendly. "There's a problem here."

No shit.

"The problem is that you've got too many books here. Most of our students don't have much money, and we have an obligation not to impoverish them excessively. We have a seventy-dollar limit on textbook requirements."

"Really?" I say. I act friendly too. "Funny. I've been here for nearly a year and no one ever told me about that. This is the exact same reading list I'm using now."

"What are all these titles? Are there any that you could do away with and still be able to cover your material?"

We sit together and go over the list of books by African American, Native American, women, and gay writers, few of which he—a Ph.D. in English with decades of experience—recognizes. I explain each text and what I intend to do with it.

"Also," he says, "in the Intro course, we do like to give students a sampling of works from multiple periods, from the eighteenth and nineteenth centuries at least, as well as of different genre. I don't see a good spread here."

I show him which works fit which categories.

Always anticipate the means by which petty bureaucrats can fuck you up.

Finally he hands the list to me. "Well, I know giving up books is like giving up babies, but sleep on this and see if there aren't one or two you could take off without hurting your plans."

I go home and call one of the senior faculty women and ask if she's ever heard of a limit on the cost of textbooks.

"Never," she says.

Then I call a bookstore located on the edge of campus, but unaffiliated with the university, and they agree to stock several of the books. I remove these from the book order and send it back in. On the first day of class I explain what I intend to do with the course, and explain the situation with the books. I ask if people will mind spending a total of ninety dollars on books and they look at me, bored with the question, as if I'm bothering them with inconsequence. I ask if they would mind walking across campus to buy the extra books. No one protests.

At the next department meeting the chair announces a new limit on the cost of textbooks. He talks at length about the necessity of avoiding too much financial strain on our already overburdened students.

The faculty sits bored with the issue, as if he's bothering them with inconsequence.

No one protests.

———

"Your contract is going to be renewed," a senior woman faculty member, who's also a member of the personnel committee, tells me. I'm standing in the doorway of her office—a good thing, since I can lean there for support when I wobble with relief.

"Sit down," she says, "and close the door.

"It wasn't easy," my senior colleague says quietly. She pauses to decide how much of this she's going to tell. "He went after you."

"What did he say?"

"He was nice about it—he said that you're probably an excellent teacher, because you come with really strong letters of recommendation from grad school, but you're just not the right teacher for *these* students. He said you're too inflammatory to create a comfortable learning atmosphere for students here."

"*Some* of the students I have are telling me this is the first time *they've* ever felt comfortable here."

"He also said that you curse students."

"Excuse me?"

She levels a serious look at me. "Is that true?"

I can't help it—I laugh. "Curse students? Is that in the Italian evil eye way, or some witch's way?"

The tiniest smile cracks my colleague's face. "I don't believe in censorship either," she says, "but it might just be easier for you here if you'd watch your language a bit."

"By the way," I say, "what the fuck is a 'comfortable learning environment,' anyway? Since when is the learning transition supposed to be a 'comfortable' one?"

———

First semester. Marcus offers to write me a letter of recommendation for my dossier, which I've reactivated in case I get fired. We meet in his office to look at the letter. He calls it up on the computer and we read it together.

I note that he's wearing his African robes today *minor crush.*

The first sentence reads, "I write in strong support of the candidacy of Ms. Kassie Fleisher." The letter goes on to detail the several times he has visited my classes, the many students he has referred to me, and the work I've done to include and motivate students of color in diverse coursework, etc. etc. etc.

"Make any changes you want," he says.

Am I going to say it? Snob! But the thing is, everywhere I go I see that women faculty are regularly demoted to first-name status, while male faculty who *haven't* earned a doctorate—in particular, my creative writing colleagues who have earned the Master of Fine Arts degree—are regularly promoted to "Doctor." So I've started correcting people *snob!* And no matter how sweetly I intervene, no matter how nicely I smile when I say, "It's Dr. Fleisher, but you can call me Kassie"—no matter how kind I am as I emend their address, they respond at the very least with surprise—and at the worst, anger. "She's a total bitch about being called Doctor!" one student writes on a course evaluation. So I've made a decision to continue to correct people, very gently and sweetly, until the day finally comes when the whole world isn't shocked to discover that women can be doctors too.

I consider saying nothing. *But it's a letter of recommendation.*

"Well," I say *very* quietly, and *very* sweetly, "it looks really great to me. One thing you *might* want to think about is changing that 'Ms.' there to 'Dr.' Seeing as how it's a professional document and all."

He grabs his head with his hands. "Oh my god!" he shouts. "Oh my god! I can't believe I did that! Oh, I am so sorry."

I laugh. "It's OK, really. It's no big deal."

"Oh, it really *is* a big deal. I can't believe I did that." He's laughing now too.

"No problem, really," I say. "When you get *your* doctorate, I'll just call you 'boy.'"

"Deal!" he says.

———

First semester. One thing becomes clear to me. If I'm going to be fired, I will not go quietly. I Sturm und Drang about it for days *much spurting of tearballs* without telling anyone and then develop some bizarre personal ethic about how you have an obligation to change a place, to leave a mark, if you're going to pass through *temporary, subordinate.* It's clear to me that this department has had a problem for some years. It wouldn't be right for me to leave quietly and force some other woman to face the same situation next year.

And leave her to think that it was all her fault.

Terminate amnesia.

I need help, but I don't know what kind of help to ask for *how does this game work?* I write to one of my mentors from grad school, attempting to describe what's happening, and she sends back a soothing note telling me that it's always difficult to make the transition from grad student to prof, to find that your idealism and altruism have little place in the practical, day-to-day workings of academia. Your reaction is common, she says.

She suggests that things aren't as bad as they seem.

It's true that I've been having a tough time anyway. The classroom is a tough zone. It isn't stage fright that stalks me, but the fact that teaching is confrontational—and I don't do confrontation. I shy *shy* away from conflict—even as I can't stop myself from cooking it up. A lifelong yin-yang *emphasis on yang.* But whatever it is, I haven't slept well since I took this job. I'm tired.

I need help. I phone the director of the campus Teaching and Learning Center. It's a tough call to make, since I don't know the woman, and I'm not good at asking for help. I ask if they keep a file on gender issues in the classroom. The woman says they've just finished a long study on pay equity and the university is taking steps to adjust pay levels so that women and men are paid more fairly.

"No, no," I say, "gender in the *classroom*."

"Oh," she says. "Well, I have some books on how women students are discriminated against. Is that what you mean?"

"No," I say again, "I mean *teachers*. Discrimination against female *teachers* and how this contributes to student resistance. How this affects the evaluation of women teachers, whether they get re-hired and promoted. I need some information about how gender discrimination operates with women teachers, and how to respond to it."

A short silence follows. "Well," she says mildly, as if I had asked about the weather, "I think all that stuff about gender discrimination is usually just an excuse for bad teaching."

I'm beginning to understand why Mormons have the highest suicide rates among U.S. religious groups. My bishop *chair* has convinced me that I don't know what I'm doing. These students, this bishop, have branded me the Teacher from Hell, the Anti-Teacher. I sit up for the second Friday night in a row, on the floor of my extra-bedroom/office, leafing through all of my old teacher-training materials from when I taught for the Equal Opportunity Program in grad school, looking for something, anything, on resistance. I'm bawling and my files are cloudy. *They hate me! They really hate me!*

I get up off the floor and resolve to see the director of composition the following Monday. I ask about my "drop rate" and he says he's never heard of such a thing, but pulls files on a few random teachers and concludes that my "rate" is not much higher than anyone else's, and that my rate is to be expected given the fact that, as a new faculty member, no reputation precedes me, and students don't know what to expect.

I go to one of the senior women faculty. I'm still new there and don't know people well, but I tell the woman that I feel I'm having gender-specific *class-specific too* problems and that the chair has informed me that none of the women there ever have these problems.

"He said *what*?" she bellows.

We decide to do a survey of the women in the department, and call a meeting of the women. "We should have been doing this all along," she says. "But everyone is always so busy, we don't see each other much."

I spend hours collating the results of the survey, which indicates that women are suffering a great deal there, at the hands of both the students and the administration. I want to release the results to the entire department but am prevented because one respondent, a graduate student, doesn't want to go public with her comments.

The student's doctoral advisor is the department chair *former Mormon bishop.*

Because of her refusal, we're forced to use summaries.

At the meeting, two new tenure-track women vent. They've just found out that the third new hire to sign on when they did is making more money than they are. At the time, both women were told that the salary was not negotiable, and so—good girls both—they didn't attempt to negotiate. The new tenure-track man has confided that when he received the job offer, he insisted that because he has a wife, and hopes soon to have children, he simply could not take the job for less than a higher figure—and the chair met him in the middle. The women want to report the department to the American Association for University Professors, file an unfair hiring claim, and have the place censured.

They also argue that they're being assigned many more lower-level classes than they were told would be part of the job, which keeps them from teaching graduate students in their areas of expertise. Then they're told they're not directing enough theses—but the way you develop relationships with grad students, thereby garnering invitations from students to sit on thesis committees, is to teach graduate courses. And this isn't happening to the junior men. One says that a course in her area was given to a man who has no formal training or publications in that area, while she is widely published and experienced in that field. Further, they've been asked to serve on a number of service committees—something else the junior men are protected from—which drains time from their writing, which means fewer publications, which means their chances for tenure and promotion are slimmer.

Both announce that they've already begun to seek jobs elsewhere.

"*Plus*," one says, "my invitation to the university Christmas party came addressed to 'Ms. W___.' *Ms.*!"

"So did mine!" shouts another.

"I mean, for chrissake, is the university president not *aware* that a doctorate is required for this job?"

I tell my story, and report that the chair did the exact same thing to the woman who was fired last year—who left quietly. The senior women are stunned to hear that she'd been fired. They'd heard she had very low evaluations, which surprised them at the time because they thought she was quite talented. They'd heard simply that she'd bagged a better job. "The evaluations weren't that low," I say. "And she's not the first."

The two senior women look at each other. "Something's going to have to be done," one says to the other.

At the next department meeting, "Gender Issues" is an item on the agenda. The department resolves to meet and discuss this matter. The chair will facilitate this discussion.

The meeting is sparsely attended. The senior women do the talking. The junior women say nothing.

"If a student has a problem with an instructor," the chair says blandly, "he or she should simply drop the course."

Am I going to say it?

The junior tenure-track women sit mutely. More to lose. I'm temporary and subordinate. Already gone.

"That's a reasonable suggestion," I say *shaking*. "But what about that conversation we had in your office about my 'drop rate' being too high?"

Silence skitters over the room. *Joggles.*

———

First semester. I walk to the door of a colleague's office and knock. "Could you have lunch with me?" I ask.

He gets up right away and follows me out. "What's going on?" he says after we've ordered.

"I didn't sleep all weekend," I say. "I'm a horrible teacher desperately in search of any strategy for handling severe resistance." He stares at me. "The Bishop called me in," I say.

"Oh no," he says.

"Oh yes. It would seem that an elusive number of students, somewhere between all of them and all of them, either drop me or complain about me or hate me and he spends all his time dealing with this mess that is *moi*. Also there was something about my having to grow taller if I want to play in the NBA."

My colleague fingers his knife and spoon.

"Did he calculate a drop rate?" he asks.

Did he what?

"How did you know?" I demand.

"Oh my god," he says, "it's happening *again*." He puts his hands to his head. "I can't believe it. I'm reliving this whole thing all over again."

It's my turn to stare at him.

"Last year he did this to my *girlfriend*. Last year they told us that we didn't have to be observed in order to have our contracts renewed, so she didn't have anyone observe her. And she had some problems with a few screaming religious freaks who have no respect for women in positions of authority, and he called her in and said she had an 'unacceptably high drop rate,' unacceptably low student evaluations, and that he wouldn't renew her contract."

"You're kidding me."

"Nope. And the thing is, there *is* no 'drop rate' calculated for the department as a whole, because if they did that, some of these fucking dinosaurs would be humiliated. And we sat and went through her evaluations and my evaluations, and the numbers—I swear to you—the numbers were *identical*. But he fired her and kept me. And that's not the first woman he's done it too, either. There was a woman three years ago, the year before I got here, and the year after that he made another woman so miserable that she just left."

"What did your girlfriend do? Did she tell anyone?"

"She was so fucking pissed off that she just wanted out of here. I think she felt completely humiliated. And like the other women, once she was gone there was this mythology about how she got this *great job*."

"Oh my god."

We look at each other.

"He's setting me up to fire me, isn't he? He wants to fire me."

He nods.

"I've never been fired before."

We sit there for a while with the buzz of the restaurant around us, me dripping and him gaping at the tabletop.

"Man," I say. "I just got here. I don't even have any friends yet. I'm still unpacking."

"You know what's really sick about it?" he says. "I went in there after he fired her and told him I was quitting too, and I explained the thing about the evals being even. And he read that as me being this noble boyfriend, standing by his woman. He liked me even *better.*"

"*Ew*, he likes you?" I say, and we laugh. Discreetly, the waitress brings me another napkin so I can sponge my face.

"It gets worse. I gave him a letter of resignation and left town. I was living with my girlfriend and helping her get settled into her new place. We had some problems because I didn't have any money of my own. And he called up and asked me to come back. Said he wouldn't accept the resignation."

"And here you are," I say.

"And here I am."

"I've never heard of such a thing. Refused your resignation?"

"Listen," he says. "Get your classes observed by as many people as you can. Try to make it someone from the personnel committee. The department lets him run free and answer to no one, but he does have to report this to the personnel committee."

"I can't believe this is happening to me," I say. *Dumb Bunny.*

"*I* can't believe it's happening *again*," he says.

———

At midterms *just seven weeks into* my first semester, the chair calls me to his office. "Several of your students have been in this week," he says, smiling blandly through his white mustache.

Grades not even posted yet.

"There is some concern about the inappropriate language you're using in class. But they seem primarily to feel very strongly that you aren't giving them enough guidance. They want more direction from you, on how to interpret the novels. It's really the *tone* of what they're saying that I find alarming—they're extremely upset!"

I nod. "I know I have a few students who are having trouble with the content, and I know a lot of them are unfamiliar with the student-centered nature of the course," I say.

His face grays. "We *all* use student-centered methods here," he says.

Uh-oh.

I've been forced to use large amounts of class time to discuss my teaching method, why it differs from that of most other instructors, and how *really, truly, trust me!* it just might be useful as one among many methods of learning. *If you've been taught to learn in only one way . . .*

"OK," I say to the chair slowly. His face is still stern.

"And as to content," he barks, "we're *all* dealing with *raceclassandgender.*"

"OK," I say again.

He pulls a sheet from his desk and shifts his glasses irritably. "Your drop rate," he says, "is at about 35%. And that is simply unacceptable."

," I say carefully, "I do encourage students to accept respon-
or their own learning and find the instructor best suited to
them."

"How many office hours are you holding?"

"Four."

"Well, since students seem fairly vehement in their feeling that you are unwilling to help, perhaps you should consider expanding that."

Yeah. I could give them CliffsNotes to scan, scrawl their papers for them—smooch their booboos and swab their rectal regions even. Sure. Why not.

He arranges his face in a placid, paternalistic smile. "You know," he says slowly, "someone who's five-foot-eleven is going to have to make some accommodations if he wants to play in the NBA."

I'm five-foot-eleven.

But I'm not a he.

"Excuse me?" I say.

"Perhaps you should make some changes so as to better accommodate your students."

I gape at him. "How many students did you say came in here?" I say.

"Oh, I don't remember exactly. Three or four. At least two. I could check my records." He tosses his hand weakly toward a formidable pile of paperwork next to his phone.

I take a breath. I smile. *Very quietly, very sweetly,* I say, "Is it possible that the source of the vehemence of the complaints you're getting is gender-specific?"

"I don't understand."

"That the complaints you're hearing have more to do with students confusing me with their mothers than with my ability to meet students' intellectual needs? They seem to need excessive amounts of hand-holding and parenting."

"None of the other women teaching here have that problem."

"They don't?"

"Not at all. I don't get complaints about them, nor have I had any complaints about the new women currently starting here. But I would encourage you to consult some of the senior women for mentoring, if you think that would be useful. I'm sure they would be happy to advise you."

———

I assumed that I'd been hired on the basis of my cover letter, which explains that my writing and literature classes have been designed to help students develop analytical skills by using writing to explore themselves and their views on social problems like racism, sexism, heterosexism *tired vocabularies . . . and yet . . .* —etc. What better way to help students develop critical skills than to have them analyze themselves in social and institutional contexts? Writing is a solitary pursuit, but is also, and ultimately, a social and institutional act. Upon arrival, I call all the officials I can think of—the Diversity Coordinator, the athletic tutor, etc.—and ask them to place students of color in my classes so that our conversations will be more productive, a bit less one-sided. Their responses are quizzical at best, as if they've never had such a prompt from an instructor.

My first four classes, totaling one hundred and twenty students *way too fucking many* are entirely white.

A sea of white, white faces.

Where *is* everybody?

weird things are happening.

common for new non-tenure-track faculty with no power to object, I've been assigned an 8:00 A.M. class.

At 8 A.M., I'm lucky if my *involuntary* nervous systems are functioning.

So there I am, lumbering into class with a monstrous travel mug of steaming, flavored coffee. I turn to this first batch of twenty-four white, shining faces, and say, "Thank god for caffeine, huh?" And grin.

They stare at me blankly.

They must not be awake yet either.

The sweet perfume of French Vanilla *dreadful stuff but sugar is a great upper* drifts through the room on the wings of rising steam.

A tough room only spurs me on. "C'mon, you guys! Does anyone need to run down the hall for a cup of coffee or a Coke? Feel free to consume the stimulant of your choice."

Blank.

"Have a Coke and a *smile!*"

Nothing.

"Oh, what the hell, suit yourself. God knows I'm usually high on life anyway."

In an attempt to help students interrogate the nature of the work they do as students, and the nature of their relationships with their teachers, I assign six pages of Marx's "Alienated Labor."

On the appointed discussion day, several of the students have not read it.

"What's up?" I ask. "I know it's hard, but you didn't even look at it?"

A woman in her early forties, a returning student, married with children, chirps up. "I took one look at who wrote it and I shut my book!" she says, beaming widely.

A few of the traditional-aged students nod warily. Better accul-turated to academic hierarchies, they know that the returning student is admitting too much.

But apparently they, too, had shut their books.

"Whatever for?" I ask.

"The pastor at my church tells us we're better off if we don't read such things," she reports.

"No shit," I say. "You're shittin' me. What the hell's wrong with Marx? He's dead. He can't hurt you."

I'm four weeks into the semester *four weeks* before I find out what they never tell job candidates in the interviews, what they never tell new faculty in orientation, what none of my new colleagues so much as mention when they ask how I'm liking it here so far.

Four weeks of jokes about caffeine, soda, and what-all god knows, before I find out.

The student body is 65% Mormon.

State institution. Publicly funded. 65% Mormon *whatever that means.*

And 98% white.

The year prior, the Mormon chair had overturned the depart-ment's decision to refuse tenure to a man who had, I'm told, few publications *publish or perish* and fairly appalling student evalua-tions. The chair argued that because the man was a Mormon, he was in a protected *i.e., persecuted* category.

The Bishop has also either fired or run out of town five new women faculty in the past five years.

But, as of my arrival on campus, no one knows that last part.

No one has noticed.

Mormon? Latter-day Saints? I'd heard of them—the Mormon

Tabernacle Choir was my favorite *after Fred Waring's Pennsylvanians* as a kid. I've been thinking about going down to Salt Lake and checking out a rehearsal ("gentiles" can't get into an actual performance).

But, you know, Mormons. Baptists, Methodists, Lutherans—whatever.

My first semester's classes go pretty well, overall—they're bumpy, bumpier than usual when you begin with a new institution, but the students are largely positive about their experiences in the courses.

But that 8:00 class. Man, that's a tough one. They never quite gel.

3.

Some years prior, and two times zones east: During my first week
teaching as a doctoral candidate in the Equal Opportunity Program
summer school—the place where I learned all this teach-the-con-
flicts critical-pedagogy shit—I walk slowly across a soup-sticky,
un-air-conditioned campus *upstate New York* to the dorms. I prefer
something of a friendly, professional distance between me and my
students, so I'd sooner meet at my office *door open*, but the program,
which is mostly for students of color, is structured on a collabora-
tive/community model, and instructors are strongly encouraged—
pushed—to present themselves in the dorms as often as possible for
forums, films, tutoring, chat.

The instructors, by the way, are predominantly white, middle-class women. Most of us are flaming codependents, an occupational hazard in higher ed.

The program enrolls two women students for every man. Nonetheless, faculty agree that a major problem in the program is the way the men almost always dominate discussions—in class, at evening programs, in the halls, at social functions, in the dining hall.

I walk slowsome, fanning myself in the mind-melter of a day, black flies nipping at my sweat.

Somewhere in the back of my head, I hear the voice of my father. A recent voice: "You be careful with those kids," he says when I tell him what I'll be doing to keep food on the table that summer.

An older voice: "That's a bad neighborhood. You stay out of there. It's not safe."

An even older voice: "Who are their people? Don't you let those kids get you into trouble. You find yourself some nice kids to spend time with."

From across the yard, I see them. A half-dozen young men, hanging at the front door, overdressed, I think, for this heat, in jeans and jackets. There are benches a few feet away in the courtyard, but they stand in the doorway. One man leans against one side of the doorframe and props one foot on the other side, forming a waist-high bridge. I can see them laughing and carrying on, slapping fives, bouncing to some distant, booming bass line.

As I approach, a woman comes to the door. She pushes against the leg of the man making the bridge. "Let me out," I hear her say. The men laugh. "Move!" she orders. Bridge Man extends his face toward her, his lips in an exaggerated pucker. She pulls back and slaps his leg. The men laugh harder. She pushes and pushes at his knee and eventually Bridge Man allows his leg to be shoved from the doorframe and she passes through. Catcalls and whistles.

The woman turns and flips them the bird. "Fuck off, bitch!" she yells.

She does not look at me as we pass on the walk.

I reach the door.

The men fall silent.

Without my planning it, the schoolmarm voice pops out.

"May I get by, please?" I say to Bridge Man.

The men look at each other. Behind me, I hear a giggle or two.

I've never told anyone this story.

"Who the hell are you?" Bridge Man says slowly. There's not a hint of smile in his face. No flirt at all.

"I'm one of the teachers here."

"You ain't *my* teacher."

A giggle behind me.

"Are you asking me for I.D.?"

More giggles.

"No ma'am," he drawls. "I'm asking you for a toll."

"A toll?"

"Yep. If you really a teacher, you gettin' paid—you can afford it."

"I assure you," I say, "I'm not getting paid enough. Please let me by."

I think about crawling under his leg, but I'm a bit old for that sort of bullshit *under is a submissive location—*

He glances at the men behind me. I have to fight *fiercely* an impulse to turn suspiciously and see what they are up to.

It's an impulse to cover my back.

And don't think for a second that they didn't feel that.

"You don't really want to get by me without paying the toll," he says, and, in a classic Hollywood gesture, pats his jacket pocket. "We'll find you no matter where you go." He looks at the men behind me and they all laugh.

I stare at the hand on his pocket. "Are you threatening me?" I say.

He leans his face into mine. "This is where we live," he says quietly. "You got no business here, and if you do got business here, you come here understandin' that you have to pay our toll. You got that?"

I take a step back.

We glare at each other.

"Fuck this shit," I snap, and turn and walk through the men bunched up behind me.

"Fuck you, bitch!" he calls after me. The men burst out laughing. At the end of the walk, I turn and see the men still watching me as they boogie into a victory dance.

I think about looking for a back door to go through, so that I can meet the students I promised to see.

I picture myself sneaking in through a motherfucking back door.

Fuck it, I think.

I turn and strut away from the building.

I go home *that's it, quit. Not the job but the effort to cross over, under, around. This is where you feel it—you feel that the recitation of episode, rehearsal of trial, needs something more than itself collecting itself, itself secreting itself. What surrounds this confession? What constitutes the circumfession, the circumstances of this confession? If a parable alone can be never-told, can hide itself, can a parable alone analyze itself?*

———

It isn't until Joe writes his way up to the second tier of academe that we figure this shit out. Academia is one of the last overt caste systems in U.S. culture; the annual *U.S. News & World Report's America's Best Colleges* has only codified and made available to the masses what academic aristocrats have known for hundreds of years *in our house it's now known as the bible. ABC* organizes national universities (and other categories of institution, but doctoral-granting programs are the ones that interest most folks) into four tiers. Basic rule of thumb is *used to be* that you'll begin your teaching career one rank below that of your doctoral institution *things are getting tighter, though, so take note: it could be worse.* From there you'll have to write your way back up.

(It's extremely rare for someone from, say, the second tier, to write their way above their origin, to the first tier. I know one person who did it. Forget it. *Know your place.*)

It's interesting to ponder the first tier of academe, especially from the dungeon that is third- and fourth-tier life. The first twenty schools *Harvard Princeton Yale etc. or some years Princeton Yale Harvard what's the diff* THE FIRST TWENTY SCHOOLS are PRIVATE schools. *Accident of fate? You be the judge.* The bottom thirty schools in the top tier are a mix of privates *Georgetown RPI Tulane* and publics *Berkeley, twenty-first in 2008, is the highest ranked of these, and six other California schools are there too, suggesting something about the commitment of California to higher learning. None of the SUNYs, for instance—to contrast California with another big-economy state—make Tier One.* One of the ugliest fights in academe has to be the annual tie for 50th *Penn State recently dragged itself to 48.*

The next 75 schools are mostly publics, mostly the flagship state universities *U of Missouri U of Delaware U of Connecticut* with a few "states" *Florida State Colorado State Washington State* clinging to rankings like #96 *eleven-way tie!* and #112 *six* and #124 *seven.* The second-ugliest fight in academe has to be . . .

After the top 125 schools, *ABC* stops ranking. The next 64 schools make the third tier but are listed alphabetically. A lot of "states" here *Kansas State Arizona State Illinois State* and some satellite campuses *Rutgers-Newark U of Hawaii-Manoa.*

Schools ranked 189 to 248 *the bottom 60 of the nation's 248 doctoral universities* are something like the fourth circle of hell. Compare, please, the difference in experience—for teachers and for students—provided by Princeton . . . and Portland State University. Seriously, I select Portland *entirely* for reasons of scansion and alliteration. Average SAT score, Princeton: 1,480; Portland: 1,050. Average freshman retention rate, Princeton: 98%; Portland: 67%. Percentage of applicants accepted, Princeton: 10%; Portland: 91%. Percentage of classes with fewer than 20 students, Princeton: 72%; Portland: 34%.

Now let's look at what *ABC* DOESN'T tell us—and for this we need the internet, an e-mail account, a telephone, an adding machine—and an intrepid reporter, preferably the daughter of a teacher's union president. *ABC* doesn't like to talk about money overtly, even though what it's doing in these rankings is . . . ranking money. But consider: Princeton has the fourth-largest endowment of any higher ed. institution in the U.S., worth (as of 2007) $15.8 billion. (Someone told me that Harvard, endowed to the tune of $26 bills, is the wealthiest non-profit in the world—behind the Roman Catholic Church. I don't know if that's true, but it *sounds* true.) All an endowment does is sit and build interest and dividends. Portland has an endowment of . . . well, they've been running a $100 million fundraising campaign with which they plan to—build buildings.

Princeton enrolls a bit more than 7,000 students. Portland enrolls 24,000. Princeton's 2007-2008 annual operating budget is $1.1 billion. Portland's is $227 million. That adds up to more than $143,000 per student at Princeton, while Portland spends $9500 per student.

Seven percent of what a Princeton students gets.

At Princeton, 40% of the operating budget is investment income. (Your endowments at work.) At Portland, 32% comes from the state government, a category not figured at all in Princeton's budget. At Princeton, 22% of the budget comes from "student fees"; at Portland, 42% of the budget comes from "in-load tuition," or tuition money paid to the institution that year.

And some comparisons aren't even possible, because people are keeping secrets. *Never tell anybody.* At Princeton, the faculty-student ratio is 5 to 1. Except for one competitor (Cal Tech at 3 to 1), that's the lowest (i.e., best) in the top tier (Harvard is a staggeringly high 7 to 1). At Portland, the fac-stu ratio is . . . well, I don't know! *ABC* provides those figures for the top tier only. Why is that? *ABC* also provides this info for all of the liberal arts colleges ranked (of which more soon), but for doctoral institutions this statistic is provided for no institution below the top tier. At Portland's web site I clicked and clicked until my carpals tunneled and found nothing.

Oh and, the 2007 average full-time faculty salary at Portland is $58,000. Yeah—$58,000. Princeton's? Skewed by the Nobel Laureates, no doubt, but $127,000. I had to dig for that last number—and it's an estimate. Yeah. If you want to know what I make all you have to do is go to an Illinois public library, and there it is. (Some faculty like to run over to the library during office hours to check and see what their colleagues are making. *I'll save you the trouble. $51,000.*) As for the private schools, that information is *not* in the public domain, even though they do accept government funding in the form of, among other things, loans and grants to their students (this while they sit on their gigantic endowments). As private *secret!* schools, they don't hafta tell.

Shh!

Money has sweeping effects. Princeton's motto is and has been, "In the nation's service, and in service to all nations"—and why not. Their endowment is roughly equivalent to Kenya's annual GDP. They can afford global aspirations. Portland's motto is, "Let knowledge serve the city"—and why not. They can hardly afford to serve a student, let alone a nation. More tragically, the theme for Portland State's fund drive caves in—*caves entirely*— to the money lie:

"Forget the ivory tower," the web site urges.

The ways in which the underclasses are complicit in their suppression . . .

One other category, above mentioned, deserves scrutiny: "Best Liberal Arts Colleges." The one I attended is ranked 44th and has been climbing for years, making my degree more and more valuable *although my GPA holds steady at 2.8—damn.* The list of top fifty liberal arts colleges is a microcosm of the top two tiers of national universities: there's a significant difference between DePauw (tied for 49th, acceptance rate 68%) and Williams (number one, acceptance rate 19%). Further, the educational and collegial experiences provided by the major, massive research schools (where no one knows your name) and the major, miniature teaching schools (where everybody knows your name) are vastly different. The workload tends to be a tad easier when you don't feel obligated to attend every little campus event, although some people despair the lack of community in the large schools.

Bottom line is this: there are 125 first- and second-tier universities, and 50 first-tier liberal arts colleges. That means that of the

3,000 institutions of higher education in the United States, most of the professoriate would prefer to be affiliated with a mere 175 of them.

Six percent.

———

In 1999, Joe and I declare bankruptcy *shame of shames—wouldn't stop giving out credit cards.* The bulk of our $50,000 in plastic debt? Professional expenses unreimbursed by our (fund-strapped) institutions: trips to conferences; printing, copying, and mailing book manuscripts to publisher after publisher; purchasing research books not available in the library—oh and, MOVING. The industry wants academics to be gypsies, but schools don't fully reimburse Allied Van Lines when you gypsy out their way—

—and job searches. Two to three grand a year to mail materials and attend the hiring conference.

Our hearing lasts three minutes. "I don't see any assets here," the judge says.

———

After a decade of brutal hours and discipline and never-say-die attitude and a solid dose of good luck—Joe claws himself up to the six-percent solution. *The second tier. His academic class of origin.* But, to return to our rule: at this second-tier institution, we're suddenly surrounded by faculty of first-tier origins. Harvard Stanford Berkeley Columbia. This is their first tenure-track job; it's Joe's second. We're in PARADISE! they're in MISERY. We can't believe our luck! they can't believe their luck. We can't believe what these people spend on a bottle of wine! they can't believe how crappy the selection is. They're ten years younger than we and far less weathered, most of them enjoying one grant after another *what they lack in publications they make up for in letters of recommendation*, which grants allow a semester off out of every three or so, to "write," and when they dine, while on leave, at our house they bitch and moan about how hard it is to get started with the writing.

"Wow," a top-tier chick says to us. "You two have an amazing work ethic."

———

To wit: In academe, the grass really *is* greener; and the greenness of the grass is all about the greenness of the buck; and if some guy tells you education and socio-economic opportunity *stay out of bankruptcy court!* are NOT about the green, just grab a copy of *ABC* and shove it right up his yummy, Yalie, sodden, sumptuous, slothful, resplendent, profusive—patootie.

———

Imagine a classroom (second-tier). There are two white students. About half the students are black, a quarter are Latino, a quarter Asian.

The room is dark, a bit warm. It's summer, and the northerly university isn't outfitted with air-conditioning. A screen at the front of the room pulses with slides of sculptures. This one is a relief depicting jazz musicians, in what appears to be frozen, stop-motion animation.

You can just about see the sax warble. You hear the trumpet tear and scream.

The teacher sits in the back taking notes.

I take note particularly of a few students who have dropped their sleepy heads to their deskchairs.

The course, in the EOP track, is called Introduction to Arts and Humanities. I work with incoming freshmen, mostly New York City kids, first-generation college students. They analyze the social relevance of the arts, yes, but what these kids really need *I'll realize this later* is the rulebook, the thing I'm struggling myself to figure out *the game—what game is this?* They need to understand how academic culture works. The things they don't know include: do the reading, get some sleep so you can think, bring your book to class, open your book, say something about the book, interrogate the book, be nice to the kid next to you, don't threaten the fucking teacher.

The Guest Artist presses a button. The slide changes.

"This is a sculpture I was commissioned to do for a school in Brooklyn."

The sculpture, part installation really, is a huge, three-dimensional abstract of slave ships.

"Hey!" one students says. "That's at my school."

Several students perk up. They make noises of surprised recognition.

You'd think they'd been thinking this presentation had nothing to do with them. That art *narrative* has no relevance at all.

"I went in and out of that thing every day and I never knew what it was!" a woman says. "It's supposed to be a ship?"

The sculptor flips through slides showing the work in progress, showing himself covered in gray dust, pouring the concrete into massive moldings *showing himself working. Yes. Art. It's work.*

"When you stand in it," the artist says, "you feel the tight quarters the slaves were subjected to when they were shipped over. If you walk into it, and stand in the middle, you feel the closed-in curves of the walls. Stand in there with another twenty people and you know what a hold in that ship felt like."

The students nod. They've been there. They've felt it.

I haven't.

He regales the students with statistics we've all forgotten: how many slaves to a berth, how many berths to a ship, how big the ship. How many died, how many were transported. His sculpture is a life-sized rendition of a typical boat.

When he's finished he turns the lights on and takes questions. What was school like for you? the students ask. Was it hard? Why did you decide to sculpt? Why do you sculpt slave ships?

One student, Asian, remains with her head down despite the lights being up and despite the discussion going on around her. She is clearly asleep.

The artist has a regal, elderly bearing. He is the former chair of the art department here, emeritus.

They listen in awe to his quiet, commanding voice.

He begins to lecture. "No one is going to help you get this education but you yourself. People will tell you you can't, people will tell you you shouldn't, people will be like crabs fighting to get out of the basket—someone will try to pull you back down, will tease you about getting uppity with yourself, will find ways to make you quit. Only *you* can decide that this is important and only *you* can ignore what they say.

"Make friends with people who support your studies. Work hard. Think hard. Think about what the system is doing to you. Think about the ways in which education is like the close quarters of a slave ship."

He stops and looks around at the students. He walks toward their circled deskchairs, leans down on an empty one, and speaks in a low voice.

"I want to tell you about something I despise," he says.

We all hold our breaths, entranced.

"I want to tell you about the thing I hate more than anything else in life."

We wait.

He grabs up the deskchair and hefts it heavy and hard over his head. He stands there for a moment with the chair balanced at the northern apex of his tall, spare frame—

and then he *HEAVES* the chair *BANGCRASHSLIDEBOOM* at the Asian student who is sleeping.

"I HATE PASSIVITY!" he bellows.

The student, dazed, lifts her head.

"There is NOTHING I hate more than a student who sucks the life out of a room and subjects us all to this sort of IGNORANCE!" he shouts. "NOTHING I hate more!"

Slowly, most of the students begin to laugh. They look at each other and laugh. They look at the student, the chair upended in front of her, its legs poking up like a dead cow.

He stands victorious at the front of the room.

The student rubs her eyes and looks with confusion at the rest laughing at her.

The Asian students are stone-faced. They do not laugh. They glance at the woman with the sleepy face, then look away.

"That was great, man," several of the black and Latino men say. They slap each other five. "Awesome," they say. "You gotta temper on you, Teach. You rock!"

"He's cool," they tell me. "Thanks for bringing him in!"

"Good-bye, Dr. Smithson!" they shout when they leave the class.

"You stay in touch now," he says as they trail down the hall.

"Ah-ight," they say.

The Asian students shuffle out silently. Dr. Smithson and I quietly gather his slides and put away equipment.

Searching myself, I find that I am entirely seduced by the apparent power of this man.

Can a parable alone analyze itself? Does it want nothing of the reader?

"What do you want from me," I asked the phone.

"Nothing," she said. And the line went dead.

But I also find that I am not entirely amused by his performance.

I won't know why until some years later, when I'll question the response of a classroom to a similar performance, effected by joggling hands.

Titsandass

1.

Imagine a small office in a long hallway of small offices, faculty digs. Loads of books feeding fleas behind closed doors. It's 1999. We're in Joe's office at his new job, mine too, insofar as the *second-tier* department has agreed to give me *temporary, subordinate* adjunct courses so we can make the rent *four digits* in an extremely expensive part of the country *fuck—four digits!* And he doesn't know his colleagues yet and occasionally one will pop his/her head in the door and say hello and how was the move and how are your classes going so far *different student body, yeah, I know, difficult, aren't they?*

Second-tier students? Difficult?

And one pops his head in the door. This is *Joe's* job, and they are *his* colleagues really, so I try to remain peripheral *subordinate* in these encounters *marginalizing myself—no one need do it for me—*

skirting up to—the edge and this colleague is, it must be said, *older* a nice-looking gentleman *paunchy* with a poet's gentlemanly beard, closely snipped, salt-and-peppered *silver even*.

As it happens, he's an idol of mine on a faculty that houses several idols of mine—a career break for Joe. After ten years of low pay and long hours, he's done it, with two books and a third on the way.

No kids for us—fertility treatment failed, and bankrupts have a tough time of adopting. We pop out books instead.

Joe introduces me to the colleague, who is cordial in his nod, but that's it for me—he speaks only to Joe. I am infringement. I am Joe's left flank. I am their oblique, while the gentlemen orate.

The subject is classes. The two have each been assigned a course perpetually scheduled in an uncomfortable classroom. They tsk their tongues over the inadequate facilities available to humanities workers in this age of fading support for public education.

Neither of them looks at me as they chat.

Then Graybeard says it.

"Well, you know," he says, a grin on his face, "you used to be able to hold class in a bar, but then the feminists came along and ruined *that* for us."

He chuckles *bowlful of jelly*.

Then suddenly he glances at me, at me of gaping mouth *yeah, still not much of a poker face* and catches his laugh up short. It abruptly switches to one of those manipulative nod-and-smile-harder things one receives when the smiler is attempting to enforce a mutual détente. As in, Yes, I know I said it, and it probably bothers you, and I mistakenly didn't bother to consider my entire audience, but let's just let it slide.

Please?

I cave.

I smile back.

———

Understand: I anticipate a sexist audience. We're all sexist. Me included.

———

Five years after graduating from college *into the Reagan recession* while working as the administrator/producer of the teaching ballet company, I decide I want to do this writing thing. I love being around dancers *everything I know about discipline I learned from them* especially choreographers, but I'm spending nearly every waking hour creating a place for other artists to create. And weirdly, the artists, in particular the artistic director, do not embrace me as an artistic colleague. I'm the money man. I'm raising the dough, selling the tickets and then *gall* insisting that budgets be followed. No, you can't use the grant money awarded for toe shoes to make new costumes. No, you can't build a new set, we don't have the money this year. No, you can't hire a danseur who charges more than $500—*no no no no no*.

The money man is the No Man. The obstacle to the fulfillment of the artistic director's brilliance. The infringer.

I return to my alma mater *strictly translated: fostering mother— foster mother—absolute knowledge as maternal figure* and enroll in a writing workshop.

I've never gotten along well in mater-daughter settings.

There's a new guy in town—it's his first semester as the resident writer. From the moment I meet him in his office I'm terrified of him. He's only five years older than me, and brand new at this job, but he's just published a book I really like at the time *still male-identified then*—Hemingwayesque, minimalist stories in which Deer Hunting always seems to feature and in which the women are largely uninteresting and overly focused on their hairstyles—"Should I braid it or cut it short?" It's in the Dirty American Realism school, the rural working classes toughin' out the snow and the rain and the breaks and the bucks. So we connect on that life-in-the-hills thing that I desperately seek to give voice to. And he has that rank of Professor, that rank, that status which in those days intimidates me, especially when a certain sort of man *masculine* possesses it.

Masculinity—in a mater context. And me with this mater complex. Of course, my mother was quite masculine. Scrappy jock. Great right hook.

But there's something else: I want to be A Good Writer. *A Really Good Writer.* I desire this more than anything. I have the sense that my prose is inelegant, inept, that the structure of my stories always misses the mark *by a fraction* somehow *OK, by a mile, but who's counting* and that try as I might *why not work with those impulses rather than suppress them* I can't say exactly what I want to say.

Representationalist realist ridiculism. Ridiculosity.

Dumb Bunny.

He knows writers. Big Famous Guys (BFGs). People who do *not* have my problem nailing a story on the mark (thus their fame and bigness). He talks about these people quietly, without reverence—which is appealing—so they're just like me after all! They get drunk and lie around in front of the speakers listening to Allman Brothers riffs till all hours—oh my! He talks about how everything is inter-connected in the publishing industry, how this person got him his book contract, how that person got someone an agent.

All of the people mentioned are men. Ergo, the network is male. Entrance to this *mater* party will be via men.

I note this but fail to absorb its implications, persist in thinking that public-ation, that fame even, that BFG-ness is entirely about talent. I'm unteachably meritocratic. *To maintain hope, remain blissful in the lie.*

I make up a long series of fibs that will permit me to escape the office *artistic director surveilling me, looking for any excuse to axe the No Man*—and rush the several miles to campus. Bring my stories to his empty, undecorated office *new guy*. He takes them in his pudgy hands and gets out his red pen.

I sit down in the chair next to his desk, focus on the low heels of my pumps *professional clothes in those days, suits and pantyhose* and the gloomy day in his curtainless window.

"Here," he says. "This is the sort of thing I'm talking about." He pulls the writing slab out of his desk, lays the pages down there, and turns so that the writing is between us *his or mine?* "Cut this and this. You don't need these long sentences—you can get along without them. See how the tension increases if you strip them down like this?"

I see. It's a slasher's miracle he performs on my tales. He takes my excess of flour and water and fat and *does* something with it, kneads it into a crisp-edged, fragile shell. He takes my stories and snips and scissors and strips them into light flakiness.

But style is not the only issue, even though it's the easiest issue to talk about. "I don't get this," he says. "Why would she do a dumb thing like this?" I try to answer, defend, explain *autobiographical, of course.* "It's not very believable," he says doubtfully *about my life.* "And I like this story about *work*, that's an important subject matter, universal to everyone—but this stuff about IUD's, about Planned Parenthood—I don't know about this one."

I never ask the key question *nor does he*: With whom am I trying to communicate? Am I writing for an audience of women? Am I writing for *him*? And to what end? To make him comfortable? Or to challenge his ideas?

"Politics has no place in fiction," he announces. "You want to write politics, write an essay."

My audience is him. And I'm *not* writing to challenge *him*. I'm trying to write A Good Story, and *he* knows what that is. I'm writing to his standards, his comfort level.

His aesthetics. His ideology.

My stories contain no politics.

What do they contain?

I cut what he tells me to cut. I curb my sentences. I see all of life in bare, slivered shards. I avoid adverbs ~~religiously~~. I avoid rebellious ~~blaming~~ story situations that might mitigate the authority of a male reader. I avoid eye contact with him *don't look at the audience.* I shuffle my feet *shy.* I dash out of his office, and out of his class, as quickly as I can. "I have to get to a production meeting—"

—so quickly and abruptly that a fellow student, another Anointed Talent who's been hanging around after class, to worship at the altar, notices.

"Why is she always rushing out of here?" the student asks as I stand at the door yanking my coat over my blazer.

"Because she's a hard worker," the professor replies, gazing at me with something in the ballpark of admiration.

He likes me!

I let the door slam sharply behind me.

It cannot be that I'm attracted to him for himself. *I'm sorry, but it's just not the case.*

He's my height. He's overweight by at least 40 pounds, most of it belly. He's cute, but in a pink-headed, doughboy sort of way *honesty—such a lonely word.* He worked as a plumber for a long time before he got this job and he wears jeans that *of course* slide down his ass, and flannel shirts that make him sweat in the coldest weather. He always seems to be around guns—in his office he spits tobacco juice in a coffee can he keeps on the windowsill *framed by ivy* and talks about his latest kill: his sick dog, a raccoon that raided his garbage, a doe.

What the hell is wrong with me?

When he makes the first pass at me, I do not see it coming. I can't relax around him. I can think of no reason why someone as talented as he would have any truck with someone as idiotic as I.

When he makes a pass at me, I'm shocked. I shake so hard my teeth clatter.

Uncontrollable, violent, physical tremors.

It's a warm fall evening.

We're both married, no kids. *Yet.*

I never thought I would cheat on my husband.

———

1998. I'm adjuncting, and have precisely one friend on the faculty, the guy who got me the gig. We have lunch together every week and we've had precisely one argument in the entire span of all our lunches, about a relationship he had with a student once. He tells it as a personal horror story. She'd been bright, talented, precocious—

and ultimately unstable. She filed harassment charges against him, he spent good money to hire a lawyer, he was forced to detail to his department chair some embarrassingly intimate details—

—and the chair let it go. When the university affirmative action officer agreed that the relationship had been consensual *that the relationship made sense given consent* the charges were dropped.

He comes to my office one day, disturbed. One of his older-women graduate students has written an angry letter, distributed to the chair, the vice-president and the president—by way of demanding her tuition money back—complaining that he swears too much in class *shitpissfuckcuntcocksuckermotherfuckertits.* The chair of the department does not inform him that he and the big boys have received said letter. The chair sits on the letter for a week or two and then, without conferring with the instructor, conducting a hearing, or even remembering (apparently) that grievance procedures *have* been established and printed in the faculty handbook, he writes my friend a formal letter of reprimand, stating that he'll be subject to "disciplinary action" if ever another such complaint arises.

"She may, with some justification," the chair writes, "formally bring a charge of harassment against you.

"Copies of this and the student's letter will be placed in your personnel file."

To sabotage your tenure review next year, the letter does not say.

Unlike the chair (apparently), my friend and I consult the faculty handbook and find that this letter indeed violates multiple personnel procedures—

—and further, that the only "disciplinary action" listed is termination.

Fuck, man. You mean you can lose your job for saying "fuck"? You call *that* fucking "*harassment*"?

Shee-it.

A month later, when the instructor's student evaluations come back from the students who remained in the tech writing course after the complaining student left—40% of whom are women—he will get a solid 5.0 on a 5-point scale—unanimous enthusiasm.

The chair will never comment on this.

———

On our first date *so to speak* we buy a six-pack and take a drive through the mountains. It's my favorite thing to do, a thing I've done with my husband nine hundred times. But my husband has left town for another job—I'm to follow in some months, after I get the company through *The Nutcracker* (50% of the annual budget) and after I sell the house.

He comes to collect me in his small pickup. A rifle pokes up from the passenger floor and leans on the seat between us. When he takes a left turn it slides from his thigh to mine.

We sit holding hands. I have a hellish headache.

"I've never done anything like this before," he says, seemingly bemused by his own self.

"I didn't think I was capable," I say.

"No one's going to lose a marriage over this," he says. "I mate for life."

"We can't tell *anyone* about this," he says. "I have to be able to trust you this way. *Never tell anyone.* A lot of people could be hurt. Really. People could get hurt. We have to accept that responsibility."

Never tell anyone. Now this *I'm good at.*

I tell no one. None of my friends, my family, nothing. It's a bleak, humiliating secret—my ugliest folly.

Why am I doing this? Body and soul howl in unison: DON'T!

We take to meeting at my house for lunch. But lunch is really just dessert.

Just desserts.

In off moments, while supervising the hanging of crumbling, snow-encrusted scenery, I study GRE exam flash cards and write in a frenzy, hoping to please him, hoping to get into grad school, where he is pushing now for me to go, a place I never wanted to go *pretentious presumptuous stuck-up snobs* a place many writers are automatically pushed toward these days *to provide jobs for academic writers?* On one occasion we sit at my dining room table *after sex, yes* while he does the red-pen thing to my stories *fuck me, fuck my stories.* They have to be really good to get me into a good program, and he is the Keeper of Good Writing, he is the Keeper of Good, he is the Keeper. I submit.

In public, at social functions organized by the English department, which I've taken to attending now that I'm writing again *now that I'm feeling real* I behave erratically around him. I can't breathe when he's around, live in terror of humiliating myself, saying the wrong thing, laughing too hard too long—so I do all of these. I drink too much and stumble home embarrassed and write in a journal where I record every word he says to me.

One night he brings in a BFG for a reading and we all go for beer afterward. In the bar later, I'm the only woman. The BFG, tired, leaves eventually, but we—the professor *Pied Piper* and his students *rats*—stay and close the bar, invigorated by a close encounter of the fame kind, by the presence of presumed talent.

Outside, in the alley, the professor jokes that they're going to have to make Kassie an honorary man.

"Soon you'll be able to piss standing up," he says.

Everyone laughs.

I'm actually flattered.

Dumb Bunny.

I never meet his wife. She never seems to attend social functions.

———

1998. "I will no longer tolerate," the chair writes in his letter to my friend, "what can only be described as your insensitive, vulgar, and obscene language in the classroom."

The colleague's intent in a graduate-level, *academic* tech writing class (i.e., *not* a vocational training workshop) is not just to teach students how to type memos, but rather to challenge students to consider how they know what they know *as* tech writers. This *can* be achieved *while* they expand their knowledge of their field, which exists right in the oily hinge, right in the fishy craw of the intersection of higher education and the corporation. Given the mess such a collision must be, he and I agree, some form of institutional critique is vital, and this sort of three-dimensional, reflexive analysis can, over time, only make students better tech writers. *To know your context is to know your work.*

Like many of his grad students, the complainant is his age, and already works as a tech writer. For much more than his salary.

From the first class meeting, she's been unwilling to question herself in this manner. She's uninterested in engaging his "message." She pronounces the first assignment "a waste of time." She simply wants to be told what she needs to "know" in order to cough up a master's degree and *presto!* get a still higher salary.

"Withdraw me from this class, and do not charge my account."

My "vulgar, obscene" colleague has been working with a search committee all fall. The chair calls him the week of Thanksgiving break and tells him that he's being removed from the committee.

When my friend asks why, the chair explains that it's political. A colleague with opposing pedagogical values has demanded to be included *equal time* on the committee.

The work's almost done.

"He's making this demand three weeks before we interview candidates at the MLA convention?" my friend says.

The chair nods.

"He just up and got pissed off at this late date?"

The chair has no real answer for this.

"At this late date?"

"It's about fairness," the chair says. "It's about making sure both sides are represented."

The only added perk for taking on all the added work of reading three hundred application files is that you get reimbursed for the trip to the hiring conference, the Modern Language Association convention that meets annually between Christmas and New Year's. So aside from losing all the work he's put into this search so far *no credit = no merit raise, teeny as that would be* the instructor will have to pay his own way to MLA, where he has *naturally* two interviews himself.

"Is this your way of punishing me for the problem with the student who doesn't like fucking cursewords?" the instructor asks.

"Certainly not," the chair says.

Students will blame the discomfort of a learning transition on anything they can find. My friend's experience illustrates clearly that in academe, it's OK for instructors to *fuck* students—

—you just can't *say* "fuck."

———

He comes for lunch *allow me to restate that.* He comes over for lunch. That is how we do it. I leave my office *nutcracker* he leaves his office *red pen at night sailor's delight* and we make our way *small college town* over the few blocks to my house *husband having moved to new job me staying behind to crack nuts* and it is vexatious, we should not be doing this, we do not know what to do with each other *we do not belong in each other's lives* there are no appropriate words, no Hallmark verses to which we can turn, there is muttering and evasion of eyes *forgive me if I can provide no dialogue* there is How ya doin'? Fine, you? Good, good, nice day. We're gettin' a great fall, aren't we? Yeah, yeah, it's a good one

Oh bother, who knows what the fuck they said to each other.

I am *don't know what causes this—every reaction to him is physiological* wet the moment I see him *cannot flinch, mustnot flinch* which is convenient since he *no flinching* has no interest in inducing fluid. We kiss *good kisser* and I lead him backwards, lips locked, up the stairs, to the guest room, a bright, baywindowed room I have painted blue, quite insistently and blatantly blue *the shade of many computer screens nowadays* in which room and upon whose bed, my old premarital bed *the writing desk and typewriter are also there* I fall upon my back, him heavy on top and we kiss, his beard velvet in places, grating in others, and he unbuttons flannel while I yank off pantyhose—we both pull off his *briefs, not boxers*—and we meet again belly to belly and he smells of the tobacco he chews (worn circle on back right pocket of jeans also frayed at hem from scraping floor because they slide down his insufficient—) and he, kissing, roots his hand up between my thighs and onto my cunt (wet) and I, kissing, tow my hand along his thigh and down his tummy and light upon his cock (wee) and he wheels himself on top of me and tucks his wee cock into my cunt and we, kissing, together pitch and reel and pitch, for a period of some *there was no egg timer* moments and *what was I thinking?* I'm thinking, This man, this man I admire is inside me, my cunt gives him pleasure and he is a hope to me, a petrifying hope—he likes me—he must like me if he wants to be inside me, if he would risk all this to fuck me—*me*—he is an intimidation, a terror as entrée to this thing I desire, he can help me in or keep me out—him as entrée, entering moi—he likes me which means they will like me *fool, you can't fuck them all*—his opinion of me matters, he likes me, he likes me, he likes me, he likes, he!! likes!!! me!!!!—

—a cry, a call, a plea—

And it is over.

No offense taken, since I don't come that way anyway.

He buries beard in my neck for a moment, then kisses my cheek. Then cock slimes out and belly yawls away.

Between my legs, mess.

He hefts himself from the bed, pulls out the chair from under my writing desk (I watch him scan his eyes quickly across the stacked papers, watch him realize that that's what it is), and sits down on it. He's sitting at my writing desk.

He scrutinizes the room *bluer than blue.*

"This is where I'm not a very good lover," he says.

"What?" I say.

"I'm not very good at the—you know, afterward and stuff."

I smile *I really mean it*. "It's OK," I say.

He sits there. Below us is street.

"Can I get you a towel?" I say.

"No, that's OK." He crouches forward, fetches his underwear. I get up and *years of habit—slut* walk quickly to the bathroom across the hall, cum dribbling already. I grab a washcloth for myself, wet it, wipe, return to the room clutching towel. I give it to him even though he has said he doesn't want it. He takes it. He pulls on jeans as I hunt panties.

He leaves the unused towel on the back of the chair. We walk out into the hall. He stops there, peeks into another bedroom straight ahead, also bright, but under-furnished, no curtains, a single bed. He moves to the left, to another door, partly closed, dimly draped. He inserts his head.

"This your room?" he says.

"Yeah," I say. I don't want him in there. I suspect he suspects that I don't want him in there. He takes one step in, looks around. For my *third-generation insomniac* sleeping room, which I have shared with my husband until recently, I wanted a dark space, a space free of stimulus *Nutcracker, Hill Street Blues, Miller Lite*. I'd painted this room a pine-ridge green. I'd wanted a room that could put you to sleep just looking at it.

He backs out and turns away.

Slowly we amble our way downstairs, him holding my hand, an intimate ingratiation I find reassuring *so I'm not a whore*. He sits down at the dining room table, where a manila folder awaits us. I go to the kitchen and bring us each a soda and a glass. We pour. He opens the folder and takes out his pen.

He goes through the story with me line by line, chopping phrases, mincing chapters. "Do you see?" he asks repeatedly. "Do you see?"

I see.

Later I'll write him a note, mail it to him at the office, that reads, "If this keeps up I'll have to cite you as a coauthor."

He sends back to me a postcard, one of those plain, prepaid-at-the-post-office things, with one word on it: "Smartass."

Before he goes, I cook him hotdogs. Before he goes, we kiss inside my door. We kiss, and kiss.

"You could almost make me," he says.

"Make you what?" I say.

"Make me go again," he says. "I'm a little older now, but I could almost go again." We kiss. "You'd have to help, but I almost could."

Back to our separate offices. Disparate worlds.

No one's going to lose a marriage over this. We can't tell anybody. That has to be understood.

No body.

———

1994. My wretched first semester as a visiting assistant professor in Idaho has just ended. In one of my sophomore composition classes there had been a young man who never spoke in class; I knew little about him save what he wrote. Never came to my office or sent me e-mail. He completed the coursework unspectacularly and left with a *B*—which was a gift.

Suddenly he is everywhere I am. He is standing in the hall outside my office. I say hi, he says hi, he walks away. He is standing in the hall outside my classroom. I say hi, he leaves. Scarier, he is in the video store. He doesn't say hi. When I see him in K-Mart one day I become frightened. He leaves, I make my way through the short register line, go to my truck—and I can see him across the parking lot, sitting there in an old Nova. Watching me. He waves without smiling. I drive around town for a while, don't go home right away, watch my rearview the whole time, but he doesn't seem to follow. My address is in the phone book anyway.

It doesn't occur to me to tell anyone about this. Every female professor I know has either been stalked or knows someone who has, and whenever you talk about these things in a professional setting, your male colleagues look at you funny. A colleague with a far more serious problem last semester says her calls to security were treated like nuisances. Menfolk seem to assume womenfolk have paranoid imaginations *just because you're paranoid doesn't mean* . . . or that we're indulging a rape fantasy or something *danke, Zigmund*—

One day he comes in to talk. "I keep running into you," he says. "Thought I'd drop by."

Uh-huh.

We chat. He's pleasant, shy, fidgety.

"Would you like to go for a piece of pie some time?" he says.

This is how I find out he's a Mormon. A Mormon won't ask you to meet for a cup of coffee, or a soda, or a beer—they don't drink these.

"Sure," I say slowly. I'm thinking that I often meet students for pie, a sandwich, the beverage of their choice.

So what's wrong with this?

But there are differences. I know all of those students very well. Those students excel in my classes.

And. Those students are all women. Heterosexual women, or

partnered lesbians. With those women I permit myself to be cranky and unlikable, so they know that She Is Nothing Special *this is what I do to subvert the transference loop of I like you, you like me, so I like you, so you like me—*

Don't like me. I'm cranky. I'm critical. I'm a racistsexistsnobbist. I unveil the worst of myself to shatter the mirror. Don't look up to me. Think for yourself.

"I'm free for lunch later in the week," he says.

I indulge an instinctive impulse to gain some leverage here *instinct*.

"Well," I lie, "I completely forgot my calendar today, but leave me your number and I'll give you a call about when."

He is nonplussed. "Why can't we decide now?"

"I'm so sorry," I laugh *never hesitate to exploit sexist practices for your own purposes when necessary*. "I have a *terrible* memory, just can't remember a thing without that calendar—and now I've forgotten the calendar! I'd hate to have to cancel on you. Where can I reach you?"

"Well, wouldn't Friday be all right?"

"I'm sorry, I really have no idea. Can I call you at home?"

He sits and thinks irritably. He's trying to figure something out. "I could give you my grandmother's number. I'm there most days." He writes the number for me and leaves.

I let a day go by, and then I dial. An elderly woman answers. I ask if he's there.

"Is this Karen?" she says.

Knew it.

"No," I say, "this is his English instructor from last year. He wanted to get together for lunch and I was calling to confirm the date."

Excuse me? I can hear her thinking.

"Do English instructors *usually* make lunch dates with their students?" the woman asks sternly.

Well, *yeah*, I want to say, but *never hesitate to exploit restrictive patriarchal practices for your own purposes when necessary.*

"Gee, I was wondering that myself, ma'am," I lie, "but I did want to be sure I returned his call."

"I'll give him the message."

I never again see so much as a lily-white limb of his.

———

The important thing to understand: I'm not really attractive. *Not, I mean, attractive enough to have warranted attention purely on the basis of the physical.* I'm not unattractive *some have said "appealing."* But *since I quit producing* it's always with the jeans and cotton sweaters (winter) or jeans and T-shirts (summer) and short hair *of no articulable color, brown, dirty brown—whatever* because otherwise it would be a mass of kinky frizz in Pennsylvania humidity/rain/drizzle/snow oh and then too there is the ubiquitous man's blazer either wool tweed (winter) or gray linen (summer) both bought at secondhand stores both big and boxy and not a very steady hand for makeup despite theater background (stage fright: never put it on myself) and no money for good shoes so sneaks or cowboy boots although when attending meetings as a producer with foundation staff there was that odd struggle with never queenly enough pantyhose *too tall* and mid-calf skirtsuits and not too-high pumps and even those I can't walk in *a five-foot-eleven fucking fashion DON'T.*

OH AND. Forever with that quizzical look, brows pinching, mouth shooting down—

A stunner I ain't.

So what is it then. What is it 'bout girls that make them so pretty/ What is it 'bout profs that make them so giddy?

What I am is . . . "Smart," people say *since the age of four*. "Bright." Quick. Quippy. *"Talented" has been used. "Gifted" once or twice. The odd "brilliant," a term usually reserved for men.*

"Talented" may be key.

He's stingy with praise *just as well* but occasionally he'll say something like "You're writing about things that matter. Work. Coupling. Important stuff—gritty." *Yeah, I know now, creative writing teachers don't get a lot of that. Usually it's the fiction about the funeral for the grandfather, or the poem about the pathos of the break-up.* Once, in his office, he says, "Kerouac said Neal Cassady had the fastest synapses he'd ever seen. That's how I feel about you."

Much slower now, and liking that.

I read his work. I like it. Talk about gritty. I read it and feel I know him *want to know him, want in, want inside the sheer masculine mastery, want to own that faculty* so to speak *that ascendancy, that capacity.*

I compliment him: *"I loved the title story."* Ask questions about where he's from, how he grew up, what he's been doing as an adult *where the work comes from.* He tells stories about himself that are similar in tone to what's in the book. I listen intently *intentionally.* Ask more questions, he talks. Ask more questions, he talks. Ask more questions *he's narrating. Us. The stories he tells* all about himself *are who we are are the sum total of mutual knowledge and the knowledge is all about him the him is. Us. It's all autobiography. We are. His autobiography. He writes us we his autography we his insignificant cock we his bowing belly we his abrading beard me au-*

tografted tabula rasa *me autohypnotized me autochthonous* I consented to this I had the chance I see *squint hard!* myself in him *you do not!* am held rapt by him *I wasn't always called smart!* who is me myself *autointoxicated, finally.*

———

1993. A new woman has been hired in the department where I'm a doctoral candidate.

I feel sorry for her because she's one of those who never did anything but academe, went straight through school *hothouse flowers, Joe calls them,* so she's very young in a department full of older faculty. Grad students are closer to her in age and interests than are her colleagues. She hangs out with the students.

This happens a lot in academe with younger faculty, and this is all it takes anymore—a new faculty member, sipping beer with a table of grad students—to trigger my Warning System. *This has been a test of the Emergency Power Abuse System. If this had been an actual emergency, you would have been told to cut and run.* I avoid this woman like the plague.

A friend of mine calls up and hints that she's having trouble with the new professor. She hems and haws and then finally blurts out that the woman has been calling her late in the evening to see if she wants to run out for pizza. The prof is depressed and wants someone to talk to.

My friend is in the woman's class. She's afraid to say no. She's having trouble establishing some boundaries with this woman without alienating her in some way that might result in a serious penalty. They work in the same field and my friend will have to have this woman's support *her signature on department letterhead* to graduate and find *"I write with my strongest recommendation for"* a job.

Within six months this woman is dating a male graduate student.

Later, she breaks up with the grad student and begins to date the newly appointed chair. Power, power everywhere.

———

On my last night in town, the last *Nut* having been *cracked*, the last truck having been packed, I'm put up by my former lit professor and his wife *in more recent years the latter being the closer friend and she, die-hard monogamist, would despise me if she really knew me.* This lit professor was my favorite, most challenging teacher back when I was taking on that last-minute English major, doing most of my coursework all at once *four lit classes at once means four fat fulsome fulminating fictions per week* the man who taught me how to write an argument paper, the man who taught me to question. *Everything—authority.* My creative writing professor also joins us for dinner. My lit professor is someone he's gotten to like in his first year at the college.

Kids and wife are to bed. It's late. The three of us share a bottle of Jack Daniels and toast my applications to MFA and MA programs (in a few weeks I'll receive my rejection from *his* alma mater). The two academics reminisce about students they've gotten into this or that grad program, people they helped get jobs *didn't know then what a feather in the cap this is.* Again, all the names are male.

"I'm thinking about going the whole nine yards, for a Ph.D.," I say.

"That would be great," my lit teacher says. "There'll be *tons* of retirements in the '90s, tons of jobs. You really should."

My writing professor *beau? former beau?* nods too. Perhaps less enthusiastically.

"But what if I don't get a job after all that?"

"Oh, don't be silly," my lit teacher scoffs, swinging his glass about the room. "We'll get you a job! That's how it works! You're good at what you do and we put you in touch with the right people."

The writing professor *former?* nods. Perhaps less enthusiastically.

"So you guys will help me get a job?" The idea seems all but wacko to me. I don't come from a world of nepotism *don't be beholden* or even a world of support. *Merit,* I think. *Merit is just the ticket, the just ticket, the only ticket. When I get something published and know the editor, the publication doesn't count. Isn't felt. As achievement.*

"Absolutely!"

They both nod.

I relax, assured that I am In The Club. I should be, after all—I *fucked* my *gatekeeper*—toll *aplenty,* no?

Actually, the three of us are overly relaxed. My lit prof runs out of gas first *but of course we are waiting him out—does he know this?* and stumbles up to bed.

My writing professor and I talk *don't ask me—chatter, the persistent vegetative state of intimidation, god knows what else. Probably another shot or two, as we had not enough of courage. Quite clearly, not near enough of courage.*

I walk him to the back door. I've decided in advance not to cry *honorary man.* "I'll miss you," I say, loitering in the doorway as he heads down the walk to the driveway, where his truck is parked.

It's cold. It's February. I step out onto the porch. He backs down the walk. A step at a time.

"I'll miss you too," he says. Perhaps less enthusiastically.

A step.

"Thank you, for everything," I manage.

A step.

"You're sweet," he says. "Very sweet to say that."

We grow farther and farther apart.

I shove my cold hands into my jeans pockets and lift my shoulders to my ears.

"Do you love me, Kassie?" he asks, slowly.

"Excuse me?"

"Do you love me?"

The voice he uses when he *as Austen would have it* makes love to me is a dense, protracted drawl.

This while I indulge a lightning-fleet bicker with myself *What is the correct answer here? Yes no yes no yes no—*

Cave.

"Yes," I say, finally.

"That's sweet. Very sweet."

A step.

Another spell of autobickering.

Cave.

"Do you love me?"

Slow step forward. Hands jammed in jeans too, denim jacket flapping open on either side of his *shall we say* breadbasket.

"Ye-es."

Perhaps less . . . *see above.*

"Would you have babies for me?"

"Excuse me?"

"Would you have my baby? I want a boy. I have girls, all girls. Would you give me a boy?"

Excuse me?

"Maybe . . . ," I say, laughing *what choice is there.*

"Wouldn't it be nice? You could live someplace, someplace in the mountains, with my boy, and I could come around and see you from time to time."

It's a joke. Just a trifling fatuous fantasy. No need for alarm.

Kick in the ass, yes. Alarm, no.

"Isn't it pretty to think so," I say *laughing.*

"Isn't it pretty," he says.

A step.

"Stay in touch." Him.

"You too." Her.

"See ya." Him.

"See ya." Her.

Wouldn't wanna be ya. Her. But not quite yet.

I return to the doorway *some warmth there* and watch as the truck kicks reluctantly *cold, cold night* into reverse *cold, cold hands,* and wheels away.

———

1993. The second reader on my dissertation committee is my female lit instructor. When she reads the next-to-final draft, she stops me in the hall and tells me she really likes it etc. etc. but something had haunted her as she read. "There's no *body* in the novel," she says. "The lead character has no physical aspects. I find myself wondering about the strangest things . . . like—what sort of tampon she uses."

"Huh," I say. "It never occurred to me."

"I wonder if it's because your primary teachers are men," she says.

"I can see where it would be disruptive to that father-daughter thing to introduce the body into the mix."

"Huh," I say.

———

February. I took two shots/Got no ducks *I love words so much because I have no language of my own*/And cold, cold hands.

Between my legs, mess.

You can check out any time you like, but—

———

1992. I've been having lunch with a male professor who has gone out of his way to support my career without my even asking for such help—without my even knowing, in fact, that such help would be necessary *he's the one who finally tells me that a game is being played, but he's perhaps overly genteel about how I should play it, so still I don't get it. I still think my people don't play such games. We win fair and square.*

It is well known in the department that he has been dating another faculty member—*someone his own size*—for years.

We have a few lunches and talk about our families and our work and the academy in general. He gives me advice and pushes me *harder! harder!* to get my exams out of the way so that I might qualify for a fellowship, which I didn't know existed, and for which he offers to write me a letter of recommendation.

He offers! I don't have to beg!

I pass my exams just in the nick of time and, solely on the strength of his letter, get the fellowship. This means that I have a year off from teaching *although I'll still work the illegal second and third jobs* while I write my dissertation. I should have no trouble finishing on time now *three years is all the divorce money can handle.*

He never asks me to dinner or away for a weekend. His intentions seem to be confined to a friendly, professional, advisory relationship.

———

At first my now-former creative writing professor and I correspond. A few silly letters are sent to a post office box I rent secretly so my husband won't find them. I memorize every golden word. I cry a lot, missing him *missing the mountains really—have you heard of* Heimweh? *a Germanic disorder* and am forced to explain to my husband that I'm desperately homesick for old friends *ten years. Ten years in those hills, my mother's sister's town, longer than anywhere. My marrow.* I write prolix, fastidiously revised *three drafts* missives in response to his notes, which are scrawled on the same pictureless post office cards—posting mine care of the department office.

I get pissed off when he writes about me in one of his novels, when he relates one of the dumber fumbling things I did once when we were in public together.

That was *my* story, I write to him—you took *my* story. *I was going to write that.*

———

1992. It takes a good number of years—five, six—to happen. I have grad school friends who talk casually about the crush they have on this or that student, their recognition that this or that student has a crush on them—and I'm amazed. Students never have crushes on me. And why would I be attracted to a *student*? I yap on about how I require a certain level of intellectual challenge in romance. Secretly—*secretly*—I suspect I must be terribly unattractive, and I'm jealous.

It takes a long time to happen because it takes a long time for me to feel comfortable enough with the skewed power dynamics of a classroom to be able to *ignore* the difference in power between us.

Some things have to be ignored in order to be undone.

I can think of two students in particular. What do they have in common? Both students are *male* my own age, returning to school after a long time of doing something else. Something having to do with social work, caring for others. First-generation college students, from the lower and lower-middle classes. Both plan to be teachers and both approach me with something like a friendly respect. They want to do what I'm doing and they like the way I do it, but they understand that I'm a girl, so the worship thing isn't relevant here. Because the heterosexual relationship is inherently imbalanced, these guys already think of themselves as my colleagues. I am quick to acknowledge their accomplishments *indeed, I treat them as colleagues—willingly infringe myself.* They approach me but don't come too close. They make vague suggestions regarding coffee—in order to talk more about teaching. They need letters of recommendation and thus it is necessary for me to know them better.

So there you have it. My "type."

I feel a pull, a connection. And immediately know that that pull contains a potential problem for all who are part of this classroom community. In fact, my recognition of the potential problems inherent in the pull I feel causes me to push away from them, to give them *less* time and attention. I scold myself that I have gone to the other extreme now: I am penalizing them because I find them attractive. I work to locate a middle ground. They are experienced, competent men who surely would not be wounded by a developing friendship with me. Still, I can see how a friendship containing that erotic undertow would change our professional relationship, and would affect the work of the learning community *classroom, graduate program, whatever* around them. In a collaborative classroom, the relationships among the students are more important and deserve more concern than the relationships between the students and the teacher. Because I am pushing away a bit, I don't feel I am doing right by these men. But I sense that I would do even less by them, and by their peers, if I went with the tow.

I never have coffee with either of them, even while I have coffee with a few women students *lesbians do not threaten me—is this fair?* I meet with the men instead in my office *door open—door always open* and we promise to get together later, but *I call it the academic nonvitation* it doesn't happen *"Let's get together!" and no one provides specifics.* I write them glowing letters of recommendation they very much deserve, and ask that they keep in touch so I can support their work in the future.

They don't *typical first-generation rookie mistake. Never cut your cheerleading squad.*

———

Eventually, it seems, he simply becomes annoyed with me. I don't know why. It could have something to do with wanting to forget a regrettable time. It could have something to do with my escalating feminism and diminishing male identification.

But here's the rub *I keep telling you, this business is about who you know:* one thing you need from your teachers is future support. Letters of recommendation, referrals to agents, etc. And so, yeah, my writing professor writes a letter toward my application for a Ph.D. program.

It's one single solitary paragraph long.

I don't know then that a letter that short will be read by admissions committees as a bad sign, that letters should be far more detailed than that. "Writing this made me remember how much I hate doing these things," he writes to me on one of those blankety-blank postcards.

———

1992. "Wanna have lunch?"

I've finally managed to find someone to agree to direct the first of my two American Literature exams, this one covering literature between 1865 and 1914. I've been turned down several times by faculty who don't know me, and who won't know me, because I won't be able to take courses in these fields *writers are lazy, the graduate director said—they have canonical gaps that must be filled.* He's a nice guy, but since I'm desperate to finish the exams at the same time that I'm taking courses *hurry up! money running out!* his most appealing trait is that he's willing to do this exam with me. "I know, I know," he says, on our first meeting, "you'll be needing a letter of recommendation from me—but let's wait till *after* the exam to talk about that, OK?"

So I owe him a little something—for his willingness.

One of my women teachers says, "You be careful with him, Kassie. You're just his type."

I have no idea what she's talking about.

We don't have lunch until I've read all 75 books, written 5,000 words in 48 hours on each of two questions he's written for me, and passed.

"Very impressive work," he says. "Really terrific stuff. We'll celebrate."

The first lunch is nice enough. We chat about books, about what we're writing, about people we know. He talks a bit about his kids, and we compare our respective divorces.

We talk about food. We both love Indian food.

"There's this new place I think is terrific. Maybe we should run out there for dinner sometime."

Uh-oh!

"Where is it?"

"Over on the far side of town, out near that new Wal-Mart."

"God, Wal-Mart. Have you noticed that they're taking over the universe?"

"Indeed."

This time I manage to confide in someone, a fellow student. Having confused myself again, I suspect that my suspicions regarding his intentions are just paranoid and I ask whether the student agrees.

My peer informs me that *she* had a consensual relationship with him.

Uh-oh!

She broke it off just before they had sex. He was a complete gentleman about it. She says she knows of someone else who dated him too.

"Wanna have lunch?"

I'm finishing the semester, starting my second exam with another instructor, and I'm wiped out. I complain about being tired and not feeling well. I've put on nearly thirty pounds since I started the program two years ago *never been that heavy before or since.* I work 900 hours a week and still have 75 more books to read. I'm not well.

"Listen," he says gravely. "I have this place in the mountains—a good place for you to rest, relax. You clearly need a break."

Uh-oh!

Say The Right Thing!

I laugh. "Oh, that's OK," I say, scrutinizing the depths of my beer cheese soup. "I'm sure I'll survive."

"No, really," he insists in a serious tone. "You'd be very welcome there. It's very quiet, beautiful. You could relax, get a little exercise."

And you know, maybe he means nothing by it. *No more than my female instructor meant when she made the same invitation, which I accepted.*

I stare down at the table and realize I'm going to have to make stern eye contact here. He's not hearing my evasions. Not taking the hints.

I look straight at him.

No small effort.

"Thank you," I say firmly. "I appreciate your concern. But I am sure I'll be fine. I'd like to travel to visit my father and brother soon and I need to ration my time away from work. So I had better not."

"Well," he says, "the offer stands. Let me know if some other time would be good for you."

I drop him like a red-hot russet. I never speak to him again. I respond politely but distantly when I encounter him in the department lounge, but I never go back to his office, and I avoid him if I see him first.

I never go to his office to discuss that letter of recommendation.

And if he is even remotely attuned to the world around him, he knows exactly what happened.

To this day I have no certification in my file that says I have done competent, well-researched work in that area of American Literature. Certainly this has diminished my job opportunities.

Two years later, the department appoints him Director of Graduate Studies.

Director of Graduate Studies.

I have personal knowledge of *three women* he has been involved with or has attempted to be involved with.

They just gave the fox the keys to the henhouse.

Not to mention the fact that as someone who is soon *knock wood* to graduate and begin a job search, I'm now *forced* to work with a director I've been dodging.

I discuss this with my female instructor—"I told you you were just his type!"—and then pay a visit to the campus affirmative action officer.

Amazingly, as I tell the woman my history with this man, I break down bawling.

I am so sick of having to swat gnats—

She asks if I want to file charges. I say no *imagine yourself in court opposite your father*. It was too long ago now. What I want, I say, is to get him out of that graduate studies position if he pulls *any* shit with *anyone*. I'll come forward, I say, to corroborate anyone else's story in a heartbeat. "I don't care where I am and what it costs me to fly back here," I say. The affirmative action officer says I can write a letter to be kept on file in case there are future problems. The letter will enable her to approach him nicely and mention that there has been a report. Which might help him behave himself.

I do this.

But the old working-class ethic twinges me. Failures aside *I've had a few*, generally I try to be a face-to-face kind of gal when it comes to bread-and-butter issues. He and I are in the same union, right? *Right?* I feel slimy for not confronting him with my plans, never telling him what I've done behind his back. Since he's in charge of setting up the dossier files, I have to make one visit to his new office about starting my job search. He seems glad to see me and offers all manner of help. He goes over my *vitae* with a fine-tooth comb. He offers to write me a letter, contact people at the schools to which I've applied, set up a practice job interview for me.

I want nothing to do with him. I want not to be beholden to him, want him to have NO POWER OVER ME.

Maybe I'm uselessly and stupidly stubborn. But incredibly, it seems to me that, given the circumstances, the best course of action here is to go the job search alone, make my mistakes *which positions to apply for? what to say in the cover letter?* and take my chances.

I do not submit to a practice interview as my graduating peers do.

Soon *I'm gone* I hear he's married again, to a grown-up. Someone his own size, someone not on campus.

For a long time I feel guilty that I never told him what I did behind his back, but I get over that *sort of*. He knew what he was doing. He knows what happened. He knows there remains a significant risk in my confronting him while he is grad director.

But still. If he's in the wrong, I'm not in the right.

———

So, OK, me and the writing prof, we're mostly over but we're still friends, right? Associates? And associates help each other out, and I owe him more than a few, right?

For my doctorate I select a program closer to home *incorrect criterion: don't get how academia works.* As a grad student, I lobby for, and succeed on getting, a reading for him at my new institution. They pay him for this, put him up at a nearby hotel. I throw a small party for him afterward. He sits on my couch, talks with my peers. Mostly it's my young *I'll forever be much older than my academic peers* male fiction friends who talk with him while I serve up chips, dip, and beer.

He doesn't stay. He uses the hotel rather than stay with me. Later he sends me a postcard thanking me for arranging the reading.

My teachers don't like him much. "The work is so . . . *violent*," my female prof says.

I've lost some points with the faculty, if not with my young friends. This is how I find out. Your associates—in this business your mentors, your protégés, your good works and services—they reflect on you. You are *who you know but also* who you support.

As for mentoring—the usual process *only recently figured this out* would be one of continuing to enhance recommendation letters, to point out conferences or publication opportunities, to plug me into the network that is the industry *this is, after all, what the boys do for each other—*

I never ask him for another thing again.

———

1990. After I have my master's, when I apply to Ph.D. programs, I look for schools with women on the graduate creative writing faculty. I sit with brochures and count names *beans* carefully. The best I find is a 1 to 3 ratio.

To get a Ph.D. in English, you take courses, you take qualifying exams, you write a dissertation. You find teachers willing to direct your exams and dissertation. You fight with the graduate studies director about what courses you'll have to take.

"*You writers,*" my first grad director sneers. "You *never* want to do the *real* work." He eighty-sixes my proposed course of study and substitutes his own, comprised of courses I've already taken—medieval studies, eighteenth-century studies, Victorian novel *all my faves but I've been there, hoped to do the stuff I really* had *missed— books by people of color, women, gays—*

The grad director has a huge impact on how long it'll take me to graduate. He determines whether I get funding for my studies. Eventually I'll need his support to help me get a job.

I'm new there so I call the woman who is teaching my creative writing pedagogy class—the only creative writing faculty member I've met—and tell her what the director said. She intervenes but he will not budge. "Gaps" must be "filled."

I determine to take the courses he is forcing upon me but to study *at the same time* for exams in different areas, the areas I'm interested in—feminist theory, women's literature, and multicultural American literature. Most people take their exams in the areas represented by the courses they take—it saves energy to read for an exam and a course at the same time. It'll be an inhuman workload, preparing both tracks at the same time.

My lit instructor, a woman, suggests that since I'll be for the most part self-educated in these fields, I won't have teachers imposing their (often anti-feminist) views on my thinking. *The bright side.*

Then. The news breaks within weeks: the graduate director has begun a relationship with a brand-new master's student who is in one of his classes.

Thus, he's sleeping with someone he has a great deal of power over: he grades her (and grades are everything), he awards her funding or not, he supports her course of study or not.

I know her. She's a sweet, young woman, smart, nice.

My problem here is that, because of his poor judgment with regard to my own course of study, I already doubt this man's capacities for anything approaching objectivity.

A female faculty member confides that *big surprise* this guy has a history of dating students.

The department does nothing. The department is host to a not insignificant number of men who have married their *own* students.

I consult the faculty handbook and find that the faculty senate voted some years back that sexual relationships with students in one's own classes would be grounds for dismissal.

No one has ever been dismissed.

The chair asks him to switch the student's status in the class to "audit," so that she can keep the course on her record without being graded by him. Not a lot to ask, really.

He refuses.

The provost invades. He swoops in, removes the idiot from his post as graduate director and tells the chair to appoint someone else.

It's a shocking move. The department usually makes such decisions. In particular, the post of graduate studies director is often a grooming position for future department chairs. It comes with a lighter teaching load and a salary boost—both of which this man will lose.

But not before he has completely fucked up my course of study.

The ex-graduate director later fixes all their wagons: he marries his student the next year.

Not that there's anything wrong with that.

The young woman doesn't seem to have many friends anymore after the news breaks. I never see her again.

My pedagogy instructor and I have a fatal falling out over this. I argue that the guy's wrong, that he's abusing power. My instructor argues that sometimes people just fall in love. The classroom is a place of love, she says—it's intimate, it's close, people come to care for one another.

I relay this debate to a fellow graduate student.

"Don't you know who you're talking to?" my peer says.

I don't know why, but I'm always the last guy in town to hear gossip.

"*She* married *her* teacher. Then *they* divorced and she married a *student* they both taught."

Uh-oh.

I write a paper for the pedagogy course, a long, serious tome in which I analyze Eric Torgerson's 1989 study of transference in the classroom (published in the Associated Writing Programs' *Newsletter*). I spend hours, weeks, in the science library reading technical psychiatric and psychoanalytic volumes on transference and counter-transference. In my paper I cite these sources to support Torgerson's argument that in the classroom, as in therapy, the patient/student transfers to the analyst/teacher their experiences with and expectations of authority figures *my analyst is the mother, the fostering mother, I should have had*. We can say in academe that we wish not to be in *loco parentis*, but society and students too often treat us like parents. Specifically with regard to teaching, Lacan has written that love of knowledge becomes confused with love of teacher. The person with power in that equation is the person who must *must!* accept responsibility for managing the transference, for making sure students aren't damaged by intense attraction to teachers *it's really the power they/I want/ed.*

For this paper the instructor gives me a B. She denounces me in her comments on the paper as "cranky and despairing."

She blows my four-fucking-oh. That 4.0 had been a great source of pride to me *something to prove after that 2.8.*

It seems to devastate her that I can't agree with her on this *mater.* She uses *her* power to punish me for challenging her own life choices. The teacher and I rarely speak again.

And I came here specifically to work with *women* faculty.

I complain to my fellow student about the low grade, far less than an ambitious paper like that deserves.

"But you *do* deserve that B," the student says, in a kind voice. "You forgot the number-one task of a writer. You forgot to consider your *audience.*"

———

Again: I anticipate a sexist audience.

———

He calls me once, and only once, over the years: when I'm finishing my master's, after I drop him a four-line note to tell him I'm getting divorced.

He sounds genuinely sorry.

His marriage persists. The requisite number of children is born *all girls.*

———

1989. To earn my master's, I must pass The History of English. Along with critical theory classes, courses in linguistics are generally the hardest ones an English graduate student has to pass to get her degree. Kind of the equivalent of organic chemistry to a medical student. Abstract, complex. A brain twister. A fucking headache. Tough on a Dumb Bunny.

I should have taken this course my first year but because I wanted to take Native American Studies courses *easily bored over-achiever, maybe, but it's a fourth-tier school; my courses aren't hard enough,* I'd put it off until my last semester, until what should have been my semester away, when I'd be working only on my thesis.

"You'd better work your butt off," my instructor says with a malicious grin. "Because I've got you now. You can't graduate this year without me."

Is it just that I'm easily petrified? That I doubt old Dumb Bunny so much that I easily embrace any *confirmation of that doubt?*

My instructor is one of those guys with an affected prep-school demeanor—he's still working the accent he polished at Choate or somefuckinplace, thirty years ago now. I know this is important because the first thing I learn in his class is that social groups without power often emulate the language practices of social groups who hold power—in order to gain access to that power. He carries himself as an oh-so-proper, oh-so-tweedy gentleman and scholar *at a fourth-tier institution.*

He teaches entirely by lecture. The students sit and take notes.

But one day, what I start writing in my notebook are the endless, relentless, off-color, sex jokes he is making.

He's lecturing about the Roman wars when that smirk lights his face again. That's how you know one's coming.

"That Messalina. She must have had a vagina of leather. She's reputed to have serviced her entire army."

Choate-y chortle.

The class kind-of laughs. The men in the class laugh harder than do the women.

When I have to visit his office to arrange for my exams, his door remains pointedly open.

Classical music fills the cluttered room. He sips from a coffee mug that advertises his support of the university's public radio station. A pipe rests in a cradle on his desk. The office smells of tobacco.

I can't get out of there fast enough.

One of my female teachers confides that he's been up on charges. She says that she's heard endless complaints over the years about his jokes in class. "But nothing will happen," she says, "if someone isn't willing to come forward with evidence."

I promise to turn over my notes to the affirmative action officer at the end of the semester and say I'd be willing to come forward, but only *after* I graduate *sorry*. I encourage a few undergraduate women students *they would be risking less* to take notes too.

I get an A in the course—fear is a great motivator, although I really *am* interested in the way a pidgin language like English develops over a period of invasions by the Romans, the Vikings, and the French.

English as product of rape-and-pillage.

I turn in my notes and never hear anything about the case again.

———

Language, learning—in our language, it's all feminized. Most folks don't want to talk about English as product partly of rape, of forced miscegeny, but as an alma mater they love. Then too, this old expression: "mother tongue." It's such a lie: we're to believe that *mothers* raped, pillaged and pidgin'ed this language, that *mothers* control "knowledge" and its articulation, that *mothers* man the gates that keep knowledge from the Undesirables.

Flash to that old Shake 'n Bake commercial—the little girl with that sham-Southrin' accent:

"And Ah hay-ellped."

———

So, OK, we're over, but we're still friends, right?

On a trip down memory lane, back to central PA, I've splurged a bit, chosen a tolerable room in an old resort in the country, but even so, he walks into the hotel room sniffing the air, squinting his nose like it's a fleabag. Not a lot of eye contact. We say hello, fall into the requisite shoulders-only hug. He's as Scots-bearish as ever, maybe even a Scots-bearish pound or two heavier, a Scots-bearish inch or two rounder.

He pulls out a chair that's been tucked under a table and lowers his amplitude into it. I sit opposite the table. Wood between us. Fake probably. Probably particleboard with a veneer of some sort. Dustless.

Across the room: the bed.

It seems to me that he's moving in slow motion.

His eyes range from one feature of the room to another *not the bed* as if he has come to inspect the surroundings, rather than catch up with an old fuck buddy.

Isn't that what the kids call it these days?

"So," he says, gazing at the steady red light on the smoke alarm, "you're here."

"I'm here," I say. "I'm here and you're here."

"Yep," he says. "We're here. How've you been?"

"Good," I say. "Got past the divorce, took the settlement money and enrolled in a Ph.D. program. Should keep the wolf from the door for a bit."

"Ah," he says, "so your ex-husband is purchasing your Ph.D. Excellently done."

He leans forward and begins to fiddle with something strapped to his ankle.

"Well," I say *perhaps defensively* watching his fiddling, "he's buying me a quarter of one. I teach for my assistantship and work two extra jobs on the side."

He's torn apart some Velcro and straightens. He holds something in his palm.

What the fuck.

"You always were a hard worker," he says. "That's what I liked about you."

Really? That's what you liked about me?

———

1987–88. A talented young woman student enrolls in the first class I ever teach, a composition class. She's smart and pretty and writes personal essays about having survived an alcoholic home life. Anything she touches turns into an off-the-charts *A*. And nice, too. She's the best student in the class and she takes under her wing the worst student in the class, a muted woman whose stated life ambition is to be a waitress—barely literate, but admirably persistent.

The talented student who takes my English 101 class then enrolls in my English 102 the following semester. She brings the silent woman with her—this latter surprising, since I had passed the latter out of 101 with a D, a grade which would typically cause a student to avoid more courses with me. The three of us hang around after class often, talking. The talented one wants to be a creative writer and I agree to alter the writing assignments for her so that she can work on her fiction.

She's an English major, so the next year we see each other often in the halls. She continues to bring in the stories she's writing for her creative writing class.

I enjoy the fact that the young woman admires me openly. That she aspires to be *something* like me. That must mean I'm *something* worth being.

She comments that my response to her fiction is often extremely different from that of her new *male* instructor. I ask what he's been saying, and from what I hear it's clear to me that he's giving the student a severely masculinist sort of read. I don't think he gets her at all.

Suddenly I note that the young woman talks about this instructor a lot, and is now using his first name.

And she talks about Tom a lot.

And now she's talking about Tom a lot with a strange look in her eyes.

One day when I tell her that I don't think she's getting a fair response from Tom on her stories, the student gets angry with me.

She defends Tom's comments, tells me how much she has yet to learn as a writer.

Soon she stops bringing in her fiction.

I run into Tom in the lounge. "I understand we have a student in common," I say.

"I understand we do."

When I hear his tone I immediately get it: *this is a competition.* For the admiration of this student. For a disciple.

He will not permit the student to love both teachers equally.

It's gonna be him or me.

I'm unable to say to Tom, *Why don't you leave her the fuck alone. Pick on someone your own size.*

So I say, "I don't get to see much of her anymore."

"You should call her up then." His tone is that of an exaggerated casualness.

I take the opening he's given me. "I try to be careful about the lines you can cross with students."

"What lines?" Tom drawls, and gives me a long slow look to show me he knows he has already won. Yes. I've already lost. *As Augustine wrote, "I am already dead."* And walks away.

Here's what I know about Tom. He's in his fifties, wizened and frail from decades of alcohol abuse. He hasn't written a phrase of fiction since he published his tenure book, 30 years ago. There are rumors that he beat his ex-wife, also an alcoholic. He has a couple of kids *boys* sprouting up wobbly.

I try to tell the student that this is probably not a relationship that's going to be good for her. I mention the papers the student wrote about alcohol, suggest that maybe her caregiving impulses are running away with her, that I've had my own problems with that *and maybe I'm having that problem right now.* But I'm too late. The student blames the bearer of bad tidings, accuses me of using her own writing against her. She never speaks to me again.

A year later Tom and the student are living together and she's raising his two children, cleaning him up after binges, letting her studies slide.

She is twenty years old, bright, gifted.

———

He places the something on the table between us and takes his hand back.

It's a gun. A little gun. Gray metal shining on the shiny veneer of fake wood. With what may be an ivory handle. I don't know a fucking thing about guns.

There's a gun. On the table between us. Someone put it there.

"What in the hell is that?" I say.

"Twenty-two," he says. "Little pea shooter. Couldn't nick a squirrel."

"What the fuck is it doing here, then?"

———

1989. My creative writing teacher at the master's level is a kind, intelligent man, refined, witty. He never touches a red pen to my writing. He writes questions in the margins in pencil. We sit in his office and talk about what I'm trying to do, how best to make that happen.

It takes years, but gradually, my sentences, pared at the fucking roots, *grow back*.

I re-embrace adverbs. Judiciously, of course.

So. You become friends with someone who talks to you at length about your writing, who thinks you have something to offer and wants to help you develop that. One night at a movie theater you bump into him and his wife and he introduces you. She seems very nice and you're glad he has an intelligent, competent wife.

You go to the library and take out his tenure book, twenty years old in this case. You read his stories when one is published. You raise your coffee mug to toast his latest success.

On some level you feel a bit competitive with your teacher, and you sometimes read his stories and think you can do him one (or more) better. You think of your teacher as a tad dinosaur-ish, part of an aging aesthetic, a generation growing obsolete. It's *you* who has the better handle on The Word, The Truth, The Way.

This sort of obnoxious, semi-adolescent, rebellious superiority *I gotta tell you* is a fucklot healthier than trying to *be* him. It's better than worshipping every dollop of wisdom that spills from his mouth and pen. Not to mention his—

For fuck's sake.

"Wanna have lunch?" he asks. This is when I'm doing the temporary commute thing with my first husband. We've decided that time apart might help us resolve our individual problems with our marriage, so I'm in school, cutting back on the drinking, and he's five-hundred miles away at his job. It isn't going well for the two of us. "I don't have a class till two."

"I'm starved," I say *what do I know.* "Let's go."

He buys because he knows I'm a struggling grad student. We talk about books, about our spouses, about what we've been writing, about the latest piece of shit that got into print and how that terrible mistake happened. We have a bunch of laughs and go our separate ways.

He agrees to direct my thesis.

This means he gets to say whether, and when, I graduate.

"Wanna have lunch?" he says.

"I'm starved," I say.

"We could go to a hotel instead."

Excuse me?

I laugh nervously as he laughs boldly.

Wink wink.

"Wanna have lunch?" he says. We're standing in front of the mailboxes with a large group of other grad students.

A few of them turn to stare.

"I'm starved."

"Though you know, I do still have that room reserved out on the strip. No one will ever know."

Eye-popping, uncomfortable laughter all around the mailboxes, my own giggling getting more annoyed.

He hits on me relentlessly, in public and in private. It's always a flirting joke. Ha ha.

I never reciprocate.

But I laugh as convincingly as I can *whether or not I graduate determines whether or not I get a job, move on with my life.*

I get used to it—I swat it away like a swarm of gnats spinning around my head.

But every time I go to his office I have to swat a fat fuzzy swarm.

I never talk to anyone about what's going on. Maybe I'm well trained in keeping secrets. Maybe I think it's my own cross to bear. Maybe I know how it's going to make me look if I complain. *No one can lose a marriage over this.*

Plus, I confuse myself. It isn't like he's the only teacher I'm having lunch with. Occasionally I eat with the woman who runs the composition program in which all grad students teach—she gets to say whether I keep my teaching assistantship, plus what I teach, when I teach *please, no more 8:00 A.M. classes, OK?* I also eat with a professor who's directing an independent study I'm doing on women's writing; this professor invites me to her cabin for a weekend away to relax. "You clearly need a break," she says. "You can get some exercise." I go, but don't relax entirely, don't *still my lit teacher* entirely enjoy myself. On Fridays the three of us—comp director, lit teacher, and me—plus a graduate of the program, their age, go for beer. One afternoon the four of us strap on bathing suits and sit in a sauna together *will they be grading my cellulite? Because the more academia I do, the fleshier I get.*

A professional friendliness with these folks is enriching to me. They know a lot about me, they have a lot of power over me. That they will make themselves vulnerable *but who's vulnerable really?* to a relationship of semi-equality with me is a gift to all parties.

Or is it?

I have these sudden moments of oddity, when I wonder why they've invited me.

"Wanna have lunch?" he says.

"You know, I'm kind of tied up today. I'm trying to get a draft of this thesis together for you. And I've got a lot of problems distracting me at home."

"Next time then."

"Next time."

I go to the woman who runs the teaching program. During her office hours.

I close the director's door.

I hem haw shuffle feet stand unwieldy.

"If someone wanted to change their thesis advisor when they're pretty close to graduating, would this attract attention?"

The director looks at me carefully. "I think," she says slowly, "that someone wanting to change their thesis advisor at such a late date would be asked to give a darn good reason."

"OK. Thanks."

Daren't do that, then.

I sit up nights rehearsing the speech. It takes me a week to refine what I want to say.

"I need to talk to you about something."

Immediately he sits back in his desk chair. His face is grave. Which means my face must look horrifying.

"Look, I am *really* fond of you. You've helped me tremendously with my writing, and I really owe you a lot. I'm very grateful."

I seem to lack an adequate supply of oxygen.

"But . . ." he says, prompting me.

"But." I suck in more air. "I'm a little concerned about this constant flirting thing we do. I mean, you know my marriage is rocky. I want us to be friends and not complicate things, and I need to be able to work with you so I can graduate. But I've gotten to the point where I'm actually a little bit scared to come in here."

He sits up in his chair abruptly. "You're absolutely right," he says.

I stare at him.

"You're right," he says again. "I mean, I'm married, you're married, neither of us needs any extra trouble in our lives right now. I truly value your friendship and I wouldn't want to do anything that made you feel uncomfortable."

"You're kidding me."

"No." He extends his hand. "We'll start over, OK?"

We shake.

I'm amazed.

He *never* says anything untoward *again*.

Ever.

Over Christmas break, the semester before I'm to graduate, the semester before my husband and I will give up *the beer, the beer—or whatever it really was that he couldn't stop*—and break up, the professor calls me at home. At the last minute, a section of creative writing has opened up—do I want to teach it?

You're kidding me, right?

"No joke."

"Do you have to check this out with anyone?"

"Nope."

He's director of the program that year. He'll tell the chair and the chair will do it.

At that school, grad students don't teach creative writing, which is offered only as an upper-division course at the 300 (junior) level. Next in the *de jure* food chain over grad students is the corps of adjuncts—lecturers, most of them part-time teachers, most of them creative writers unable to get full-time work (a situation in which I'll soon find myself)—who have their degrees and work for misery pay but often find that, when *de jure* is not the *soupe du jour*, the department favors graduate students over them despite their degrees and experience. *Think back to those ABC rankings. High number of grad students: good thing. High number of adjuncts: bad thing. Ergo: grad student happiness matters; adjunct happiness, not so much.* Generally, upper-division classes are saved for tenured and tenure-track professors.

So, no master's candidate has ever taught creative writing at that school.

Also *and sorry, but this is an issue* no woman has *ever* taught creative writing at that school. The permanent creative writing faculty has always consisted entirely of men.

It takes some juggling of schedules, but I accept, gleefully. Here is a chance to work in my own field, to try out some of the ideas I've been collecting about reforming creative writing pedagogy.

Great news, right?

A group of male adjuncts are enraged that I've been assigned this course instead of them. A friend of mine, another lunch buddy, leads this group. He goes to the university's affirmative action officer and files charges, argues that the male part-timers outrank me in experience, degrees, and ability, and that they are being discriminated against because the director of the program and I are having an affair.

We're WHAT?

"Well, everyone can *see* it," he says into the phone when I call him to find out precisely what the *fuck* he is *doing*. "We can see what's going *on*. We know your marriage is ending" *it IS?* "and we see you two in the office, we see you in the lunch room."

"*Nothing* is going on," I say. "He used to make passes at me all the time, but I talked to him about it and he *quit*."

"Look," he says, "this is nothing personal. It's got nothing to do with *you*. But this guy has always been like this—he's always hitting on some chick or another, and I know plenty of women he *did* sleep with, for years now. He has to be stopped."

"He has to be stopped?" I ask. "Or *you* have to teach this *course*?"

"He has to be stopped."

"I had no idea you were such an advocate for women's issues in the university," I say. "If he's been doing this for *years*, then by golly it's a darn good thing we're going to stop him *now*."

There's a rumor that my professor and I will be called to the affirmative action officer's hearing and I think maybe we should get our stories straight. I call him at home, something I've done only on rare occasion.

His wife picks up the phone.

"Hi, this is Kassie."

"*Ah, yes*," she barks. "How *nice* to *talk* to you. Fine *mess* we have here, *isn't it?*"

Silence. I mumble something.

"Well," she says, "I have told him and *told him*, this is what *happens* when you have lunch with women students. I hope you're both *satisfied*."

"Please tell him I called," I blurt, and hang up.

It's a full-blown *quelle scandale*. Every time I walk into the lounge where grad students and adjuncts hang out, everyone stops talking. I'm sure I'm not imagining this. It happens over and over. I walk into the small lunchroom where most of us go for salads and sandwiches at noon, and whole tables fall silent as I walk by.

It gets so bad that when I'm invited to the home of a friend for his every-semester bash to celebrate the start of a new term, I'm actually grateful merely because he hasn't excluded me.

When I arrive, that scene from *Gone with the Wind* plays out, where Scarlett walks into Melanie's party in that tarty red dress after she's been caught sucking Ashley's face.

A hush collapses upon the living room.

In good Melanie form *thank god* my host marches right up to me.

"Kassie, you're looking marvelous. What would you like to drink?"

"Whiskey, thanks. Leave the bottle."

He takes my arm and tromps me through the silent mouths and into the kitchen.

My host and I look at each other and burst out laughing.

On Friday, during beer, the woman who runs the teaching program says, "I had no idea this was going on."

I had only dropped her, oh, 900 clues or so.

"So this is why you asked about changing your director."

I tell her all of it. That I had gone in and talked to him and he had changed completely overnight.

"I'm really impressed with you," she says, as if she really *is*. "It's incredible that you did such a good job of saying exactly the right thing. You handled it just right."

I know the woman is trying to be supportive, but I'm shocked at her.

If you *credit* the victim who manages to fight off an assault, then you have to *blame* the victim who *fails* to do so.

As it happens *accident? You be the judge* this comp-program director had an affair with one of *her* instructors while she was a grad student. In the same way that academic departments are often populated by men who have married former students *or at least had a fling or two* departments also contain women who have slept with a teacher *rarely that married thing, though.*

I lose at least a half dozen friends over the scandal—particularly the "friend" *nothing personal* who led the male part-timers' revolt.

After meeting with the male adjuncts, the affirmative action officer throws the case out.

———

"Kassie Kassie Kassie," he says. "Been a looooooong time. So. You're getting a Ph.D. You're going to be one of the smarties."

"I'm trying to. I don't know if they'll give me one. They think writers are stupid. They're making me take extra classes to 'fill gaps.'"

———

"Fucking paper pushers," he says. "Fucking orderers of paper clips. Don't know shit about art. They're all the same."

"How's work for you?"

"Same old same old. Students crave the glory of my red pen. Colleagues avoid me. I have one friend there. That's about all you can expect in any given department. He and I hang out." He crosses his chunky legs and fiddles some more with what I have concluded is a holster around his ankle uh . . . Miami Vice *this ain't. Really.* He presses the Velcro together, tears it apart, presses it together again.

"And how are the girls?"

"Girls are great. They're great. The little ones are doing great in school. The wife is in grad school now, too. All these women getting advanced degrees. What's *with* that?"

"You have an MFA."

"Yeah, but I barely cracked a book for that. I wrote a bunch of stories and got drunk and did a little plumbing on the side. She actually *studies.*" He lets go of the Velcro and places his hand on the gun. Fiddles with it for a moment.

Wow.

It's over. Entirely over. The two of us can hardly stand each other.

So this is where this shit leads. An out-of-the-way hotel room, a gun that doesn't go off in the third act. The shriek of Velcro peeling on and off, on and off.

2.

Imagine a Reluctant English Major, enrolled in a seminar on Romance Literature. Beowulf and the like *gak*. Our instructor has assigned John Fowles, whom I'd already discovered by then and adored *then*. No women writers are on the reading list, because Romance as Literary Category is worthy of Critical Analysis only when Men Write It.

Not that I knew that then.

1981. The instructor is young-ish, this or that side of thirty—hard to say because he's balding, throwing off the estimate. He's not good-looking *does the phrase Bozo the Clown mean anything to you?* but he's casual and charming and has nice eyes and doesn't try to lord it over his students—he talks to us like we're actual adults, like he likes us, and this is what makes him attractive *he likes us we like him he likes us an endless feedback loop of accelerating affection in-terruptible only by challenge—like, say, what if I raised my hand and asked why there are no women on the reading list? Would you still love me then?* We relax around him, think he's cool. The course is pleasant *not terribly demanding.*

Spring fever *spring was late in coming that year* hits the campus annually like an epidemic. We all go a bit nuts and it becomes harder than usual to stick to the books.

Spring was late in coming that year.

Professors surely suffer from the budding of dogwoods as much as do students. So one fragrant Wednesday afternoon we gather around the heavy oak seminar table and sniff at the open, green-ing windows and natter and desperately want to be out there, not in here. And at the appointed hour, the instructor walks in. He's cheerful, chatty. He sits toward the back of the room and yaks with us about the weather, about Spring Festival.

Then he turns his attention to one student in particular. She's one of the beautiful kids, one of the sorority girls I can't even speak to—medium-smart, classically dressed, quiet, modest, gig-gly, pretty, shiny-haired, minimally but always made-up, pinned. She never has my bad friz days. She never looks tired or depressed. One of her sweaters costs what all of my T-shirts put together cost. She wouldn't be caught dead in the faded, men's corduroy jeans I'm wearing. Unlike me, she wears sneakers only for jogging, an activ-ity she manages without excreting a drop of sweat. Her boyfriend's family probably built her dorm or something.

"So Catherine," he says breezily, "you want to get together for racquetball again tomorrow?"

All eyes yank to Catherine, whose face immediately goes pinker than her mohair sweater, too warm for this weather.

He grins from his laid-back perch in his chair. Waiting.

"Sure," she says finally.

"Three o'clock still good?"

She manages a nod.

"OK, my turn to reserve the court this time."

I stare at him, stunned. We all do. Catherine fusses at her hands until discussion is well underway, when she begins to take notes. I don't remember her speaking in class much anyway, but she certainly ventures nothing that day. I suspect that jealousy, which mosquito-fogs the room, closes shut the woman's throat. She can't have missed that stab the rest of us feel, followed quickly by stabs of something faint *is it anger?* at him *and her—that's the lethal part of it: AND her.*

I'm *forever* out of the gossip loop—I don't hang out with the right kids to know about this sort of thing, and I'm too buried in my books, my family, my own scribbling, my own shit, to pay attention. I've heard a few stories. There was one young woman, a fellow theater student, an eccentric and flamboyant actress from New York who complained endlessly about the Appalachian backwater in which she treaded—"This water—I can never get the shampoo out of my hair!"—who told me, one night after a long rehearsal, that she'd wrestled on the office floor of our American Drama instructor. I knew his wife, so I thought the actress was making it up. *I actually thought that professor + wife = monogamy. Professors being, you know, hallowed beings of enlightened behavior towering some miles above my own family. What a Dumb Bunny.* I'd also stumbled onto a rumor about a professor in another department, also married, who'd written a student an angry letter when she broke off their affair—a letter complete with unfortunate references to "cockteasing cunts." Said student had turned said letter over to the dean as Exhibit A. The dean had had a few things to say to said professor. *No—he wasn't fired.*

It turned out that my Romance instructor was not dating Catherine. In fact, he had been dating Catherine's best friend—someone equally sorority, pretty, rich, etc.—but more artsy. She was a talented poet. In fact, she was The Other Writing Student upon whom my creative writing instructor doted. We were the two Anointed Talents among our writing classmates *there are always two—what must the rest think of us*? We competed with each other from afar, maintained a resentful distance from each other.

I knew nothing of her relationship with the Romance Lit instructor.

The pair married right after graduation.

———

1990. I make a friend. A poet from another country, whose day job is not academia. She's a graphic artist, writes in off moments, enrolls in writing workshops at a nearby university.

She's involved with hers too. Her writing teacher. He's a BFG in their country, married to an academic who teaches at a university far, far away—far enough to allow him to waltz out of wedlock.

And actually, I meet this friend in an interestingly roundabout way. A colleague of mine slept with this selfsame BFG moons and moons ago when my colleague was his student. My colleague thought I would like to meet him, and, when we all were at a conference together, arranged for dinner. BFG brought along his current student flame. The poet.

So. Another recidivist.

And I do like the BFG—a sweet, sweet man *older and paunchy but attractive* and brilliant, far more brilliant than a Guy has to be in the United States to become Big and Famous. Talented, too *it never ends: I've read his best known work in preparation for the dinner and am appropriately complimentary—but has he read mine?*

Understand: I anticipate a sexist audience—but also, perhaps— dare I say—an elitist one. One that might ask why a BFG would bother with work by a Dumb Bunny.

Despite pre-preparation for an audience with the BFG, the person at table I really click with is the flame. Bright, curious, interesting *christ, someone who doesn't talk about students all night and day!* Peppers me with questions, which I return. Writes me a note after we each depart for our home countries—which note I return.

And thus is born a staggering correspondence.

We've spent little time with each other but we are girlfriends to the death. We tell each other everything *about the lovers in our past, and why they didn't last* . . . As it happens, our teacher-beaux have the same first name. We refer to them as The F___s. We share work and *potentially tense moment* find *relief* that we like each other's work a great deal. The poet has a hawk's eye for detail, a comely ear for language, and seems to enjoy the tales I unfold in my fictions.

But the most important thing we share is that we are both *as Austen would have it* connoisseurs of human folly. This is what sparks our correspondence. We regale each other with the ridiculous antics of our relatives, our friends, our coworkers, our lovers. The letters grow longer and longer as the years pass—twenty, thirty single-spaced pages. It takes me days to write mine, and when one arrives from the poet I wait until I can give it fit attention, then consume it utterly. My poet friend is a marvelous journalist, in the original sense of that term. She misses nary a twitch of particulars as she narrates the latest dinner party fracas.

Also. I'm almost done with my F___ when the poet and I meet— almost but not quite—while the poet is still deep into hers. As time passes, the poet begins to feel that she has to escape what has become a calamitous engagement for her. She needs her time and psychic energy back. She needs publishers to see her as something other than her F___'s latest long-distance arm candy. When the entire community goes to F___'s wife's university for a conference, she is excluded. F___'s friends reject the paper she proposes to give at the conference, thus protecting F___ from himself by preventing a face-to-face between the wife and the flame. She's tired of picking him up at the airport, doing his laundry, making sure his local rent is paid while he's on a book tour. Socializing with his colleagues when she has no socially acceptable status at table vexes her. She's irritated by sleeping always at his place, never being in her own home, by line-editing his galleys, and particularly by his comments on her work *Always the same, she said. Am I not evolving, she said, or is he entirely stagnant? Is either one of us moving? Is my work altogether derivative of his, as everyone says it is? Is he, in fact, writing it? As everyone says he is? Without my apprehension of this fact?*

But it's painful. She imagines herself to be in love, she says. It's impossible—he won't leave his wife. And he's done it so many times—is it really true that she's different from the last dozen? That he really does love *her* more, need *her* more, than the earlier ones? Perhaps it's his age, she says. He's past sixty now *a thirty-year age difference* and feels mortality breathing down on him.

She tries to break up with him. He doesn't want to lose her, carries on about it. They reconcile, they "try," he promises to consider leaving his wife *his fourth*. He agrees to take a cab from the airport, she insists that he stop reading her work—they ping-pong, yin-yang, back and forth until finally—

It's over.

The poet and I postmortem the situation. What is it they see in us? We're not agonizing to look at, but tens we're not. Ladies in red we are, decidedly, not. And still they come *over and over, even as we come not at all.* We've heard of students who make the first move but in both of our cases such has not been the case. *What do they want from us? Why did we say yes?*

But it's not always useful to think in terms of intention. Yeah, so some of it's transference—dumb bunnies put the BFG's on a pedestal, we're attracted to the power, we want access to the power, this while they want to be pedestalized, they desire to control that desire of ours, they want in fact to own our pedestalization so much that they desire to shove their pedestal *into* us. It's all about power—almost too easy an equation.

We have to look at results, rather than intention, because ultimately—and much as we might experience it as otherwise—power is not a commodity. It's a dynamic, a fluctuating configuration, and eventually between any given pair the tectonic plate shifts. Either of us can withhold the fucking, unhinge the approval, descend the pedestalizing. So intention is not the most productive part of this equation.

To wit, the results: The results are that the female apprentice *can't speak for men and gays and lesbians—I'll let them tell their own stories* the apprentice ends up with nothing. Even if the professor has good intentions and *makes an honest woman of her (will you look at this rhetoric!)*—even if the professor marries her, she ends up with far less than she may deserve. The history of women's writing reaching back and back through millennia *research it yourself, why don't you* is that any excuse the public can find to denigrate a woman's writing will be used. *He's the brains of the operation, he wrote it for her, well OK then he edited the hell out of it, it was originally his idea, she wouldn't have gotten it published if he hadn't pushed his connections with the publisher, she wouldn't have gotten those reviews if he hadn't coerced his friends, she wouldn't have gotten a reading if he hadn't pressed the bookstore owner, she wouldn't have gotten her panel accepted at that* other *conference if he hadn't known the organizer, his old grad school buddy got her that teaching gig, all of her acquaintances in the industry are really his, she's a great cook and really good with people but folks actually go over there to listen to him talk . . .*

I mean, you get it, right? *Joe* actually wrote this book. *The Autobiography of Alice Down The Bunny Hole, As Seen Through A Glass Dumbly.*

And that, the poet says, is the *best*-case scenario. If he doesn't leave his wife and waltz you away to a honeymoon, that means the relationship ends. When the relationship ends, the power polka peters out. There's no incentive for him to remain engaged; in fact, there is every disincentive. That means no mentoring. That means no letter of recommendation. No help getting a job long-term. No help getting published. *No help becoming a better writer.* And it's not just him: it's all his friends. And since he's been mentoring you, your connections are his connections—but systems are no longer go, since his friends feel as awkward about your erotic/aesthetic demotion as does he. *They may actually be relieved to see that he's cleaned up his act: they can look his wife in the eye now. Well. For a while.*

What that means, sayeth the sooth, is that they fuck us away. They remove us as potential conflict partners. You have to compete in this game, for jobs, publications, reviews, speaking opportunities—they fuck us right off the board. They pick the most talented girl in the class *our adoration would be worth little if they thought us giftless boobs* and fuck her out of existence. Fucking erase us. Fuck us to fragments. Fuck us to extermination, ruination. And the extra bonus point is that they leave us with bullshit crap-hole self-esteem. With the fucking over *fucked-over* we have no one to tell us, however mutely, that we're talented. The business is all about who you know and we know nobody now. So the poems sent cold over the transom to the editor, a stranger to us *and he too mostly publishes who he knows*, come back with slips of papers attached. "Not right for us at this time."

Oh, sure, one or two of us might end up with the real deal. A happy family, and/or public. That's one or two of us out of every . . . ten? twenty? thirty? But the rest of us?

"Us." Who's "us"? We ain't *it*, baby. Us *was* them. And they cut us off just before we got any better than they are. *Perhaps that is our ultimate crime. Talent. Smarts. Broader than theirs because practiced more, for survival.* Ideally, a mentor's protégé goes on to do him one better *child outreaches parent*. But rare is the mentor *mater* who has no problem with that—or who, assuming we all suffer from this (and we do) *feels* that envy but doesn't act on it. Oh yeah, and then we reread their work and notice, for the first time, a goodly dose of misogyny contained therein. Out there in Deer Hunting country. Huh. How come we didn't notice that before? Power, or promise of, masculine power made us blind. Power rendered us lousy readers. Critical thinking *question authority* is out the door.

Or, this experience has *tripled* our capacity to see power, and we're *way* better readers. But to what avail?

Final answer?

We were whores.

Congratulations, you fucking, fucking idiot. You fucked yourself off the map.

Nice going, cunt.

Now. Return to Square A. Begin again, from the beginning, forearmed this time with a fucking clue. See if you can keep your jeans zipped this time around. See if you can keep yourself from *erasing yourself* off the game board.

Increase Emergency Power Abuse Threat Level to red. Leave it there permanently.

———

At a conference, I run into a colleague of his, hear some rumors about him.

Someone needed something from his office, knocked, waited, heard nothing, knocked again, walked in, and found him *in flagrante delizioso* with a student.

And this would have been a traditional-age student, eight years younger than I was then.

Not that my age had brought me any particular maturity *silly silly wabbit*.

Another student brought charges against him for sexual harassment. It was mediated and (presumably) he agreed to behave and the charges were dropped.

Note to self: this would have been during the same period when he was becoming . . . annoyed . . . with me.

So in retrospect, I turned out to be merely the *first* student he slept with during his *first* year at his *first* job. I turned out to be the oldest in a long line.

I am the progenitor. The avatar.

If I'd said no, would it have been harder for him to start down that road? With much younger women to come?

———

The whole time I'm in college, I study with precisely *two* female instructors—one in theater, and one in English.

(No people of color. A Southeast Asian man is on the English faculty, but students complain about his accent and I avoid him *stupid*.)

As for male teachers, two stand out in my memory. I take two Am Lit courses with a wonderful man who, with a tremendous and irritable *perhaps crazy even* persistence, accuses me of being "lazy" and teaches me what I don't know about writing and revising by first announcing that I'm not the great writer his colleagues think I am. ("Just because you have the gift of being able to put a SENTENCE together doesn't mean you're SAYING anything in that sentence!") He assigns books steeped in masculine conquest motifs, by James Fenimore Cooper and Mark Twain and Daniel Boone. It's whispered that he's a "Marxist." I don't know what that means, but he's cranky as hell and I can relate to his irritable *working class?* behavior—even as he slashes my papers with red ink *("You call this a THESIS?")* and awards me—gasp!—a C in Frontier Lit.

He really pisses me off. But I can see how I deserved it.

That's called real *teaching.*

I have a bit of a crush on him.

Timidly, meanwhile, I approach the office of my very gruff, very handsome, very charismatic Drama instructor, who, as noted, enjoys the odd roll with women students. I've been struggling—valiantly, I assure you, during my brief, senior-year stint as A Good

Student—with a paper on O'Neill that has to do with his use of time, the way his plays unfold in what seems to be real time, but can't be. I deeply desire this instructor's applause and hope to produce a work of virtuosity sufficient to attract his notice and mutual admiration. But after several stammering drafts I am way the fuck up against the next day's deadline—desperate—and see no alternative but to confront my fright and ask for help.

My knock is barely audible.

"Yes?" he barks. He does not ask me to sit down.

I fumble hem haw and bubble out my thesis, stare at the carpet, fidget my feet.

He rises up brusquely from his stacked and scattered desk. "It sounds like you might be onto something there, but it's a bit late to be asking about this now, isn't it?" He menaces me with two armor-piercing bullet-eyes. "Well, isn't it?"

"I'm sorry," I mutter.

He pushes past me and out his own door, leaving me standing there alone. In his office.

Huh. How do these guys get away with this shit, and still collect high teaching evaluations—disciples, even? If I did that . . .

That evening I pull an "all-nighter" and bang out, in one draft on Jane's Smith Corona, a standard fifteen-page paper on characterization in Albee's *The Sandbox*. I could have done it in my sleep but I manage to stay awake till five.

Two weeks later he returns that dull, done-a-million-times, un-revised paper with an A-. I'm immensely relieved and on my evaluation of his course declare him brilliant.

The fact that I fear my (male) teachers makes all the more re-markable the fact that I actually have dinner! with one of my two women instructors *no fear there* and frequently visit the office of the other *no fear there.* The former of these female instructors is young, just beginning her career, and is only temporary to this campus, replacing the theater department head while he takes sabbatical to write his book—so, yes, she has no authority. One night, while I'm stage-managing her show (*The Man Who Came to Dinner*), she cooks for me in her quaint, pint-sized, temporary apartment—and all I remember about that night is how apprehensive I am, how inelegant I feel, how overawed I am by her *trifling, I now see* academic rank *it's a visiting for chrissake.* I recall, as if it were the day before yesterday, how endlessly I fiddled with her modest eating utensils, her economical linens *as if I were sitting in Bookbinder's.* I do a good job for her *backstage is my natural-born platform* but we don't spend any time outside of the green room again. Certainly she thinks me an utter dolt.

But *understand: this is progress.* I wish to perform well for a female instructor and am willing to work for that approval. I'm willing to learn from her, willing to humble, to subject myself *people don't get this—to learn is to be humbled—humility is the most necessary part of learning* to her. I subject myself to a *her.* Yes, I'm feeding myself into a transference loop, but at least I'm willing to trust her *a her* that *itty-bitty* much.

Meanwhile, back in the English department, where we theater students take drama-as-literature courses, my Renaissance Drama instructor is a tall, pantsuited, willowy vision with gray-streaked hair, a dry, sardonic humor *just like mine* and a smartass smile that almost always decorates what is really a very pleasant face. She has beautiful skin.

I can't stand her.

Her lectures bore me. I find her completely unattractive. I can think of no reason to read *The Duchess of Malfi* and I come to class sighing and irritable, slap open my notebook, slump my head on my hand and take half-assed notes as she talks. When she spices her comments with an interactive question, just as all of my male professors do, I decline to favor her with a reply. If she becomes frustrated at the lack of class engagement and calls on me, I reply drowsily and as if I cannot even begin to fathom what she could mean—as indeed I cannot, because I simply refuse to think *for her.* I find her wildly uninspiring and unmotivating.

Her office door is open. Inside she sits with another student *male, naturally* talking. I bang confidently on the open door and wait expectantly.

She looks up at me through glasses. "Take a number," she says with that sharp, tilted smile of hers. "We'll be right with you."

She and the student are discussing the difference between *The Beggar's Opera* and *The Threepenny Opera*, and whether Bobby Darin would have been well cast to sing "Mack the Knife" in the eighteenth century.

I'm a Bobby Darin *freak*, but even this discussion finds me leaning on the doorframe, yawning cavernously.

When the student leaves, he nods at me with razor-edged precision, irked that I am crowding him out. I walk through the door without invitation and drop onto the warm chair.

I desperately need my ass kicked.

"Next!" she calls, though I am already in the room, seated. "Just like the dentist," she says wryly. "Have you been brushing and flossing and practicing good oral hygiene?"

I glower at her. She cants her desk chair back and tucks her hands behind her tidily trimmed head. I lean forward and prop my elbow on her desk.

"I'm having trouble coming up with a paper topic," I announce.

"Really," she says, looking at me over the rims of her glasses.

I wait expectantly.

"Well?" she barks. That half-smile *willpower* is still in place.

"Well?" I bark back. "I'm not sure what I should write about."

"OK. Which of the works interest you?" she says.

Annoyed, I shake my head.

"Look," she says, "you don't have to like a work to write about it. Aren't there any aspects of the works you want to ask some questions about?"

Again with the head shaking.

She stares at me evenly for some time. I stare back.

Bang-down comes her chair. The half-smile is gone. "I can't help you," she says flatly.

"Excuse me?" I say.

"I can't help you. You need to dig into this reading and discover something for yourself. I can't hold your hand for that. If you come up with a topic and you want some help developing it, please do come back."

"But I don't know what to do!" I protest.

"I'm sorry to hear that. I'm sure you'll work it out if you give it some thought."

I stand up. "Thank you for your time," I say bitchily.

"Indeed," she answers. "Good luck to you."

I have absolutely no memory of the piece of shit I handed in to her, but she gives me a *B* for the course—a gift. On my evaluation of her I pronounce her utterly callous and unhelpful. I remember almost nothing about Renaissance Drama except how exhaustively dim I found that era to be. *If only I'd known then what I know now about, say, Aphra Behn . . .*

So.

Every time I get a vacant, irritable student in my class; every time a student knocks on my door expecting me to wipe her ass for her; every time a student is turned away by a male professor who says he has no time for her, and she comes to me, assuming that I have all the time in the world; every time a student just isn't interested in my approach to things, just doesn't feel like doing the reading I assigned—every time—

3.

Imagine a job search, 2001 or so. You're on the inside of this one, a fly on the drywall, an ear to the background. A creative writer is needed and the department cedes to members of the creative writing program the task of collecting a pool of four finalists. There are only two women among the writing faculty and, with the prodding of the program director (one of the women), the group agrees that they need to hire a woman. They dust off the usual bag of tricks and append "preference for candidates with a background in women's lit" to the ad. They get a decent crop of candidates and all of the finalists, invited to campus for two-days-long interviews, are women.

Now that four invitees have been selected, the entire English department faculty will be asked to approve whichever candidate the creative writing program recommends.

None of these women are feminists, or at least they don't indicate same, either in their published work or in their lectures. Their writing isn't particularly challenging in conceptual terms. In fact, during her job talk, one candidate *turns out writers can be stupid after all* makes the typical creative-writing, anti-intellectual crack, asserting that to be a good writer one is best off remaining . . . stupid. "Don't think about that incomprehensible postmodern crap—just hit the ball." An entire roomful of professors *the people who get to choose* have a nice smirky heroic-author-culture chuckle at this.

After the on-campus visits, the creative writing faculty narrow things down to two people—and hit an impasse. Two of the older men *within earshot of retiring but nonetheless forcing their biases on the next thirty years of institutional history* pull for the most attractive candidate. Two *a man and one of the women* pull for the smartest *relative concept*. The director of the program had been pulling for the one with the most awards/status/prestige, but, having missed the others' presentations, has no opinion about the others and therefore can't vote.

Why not? Where were you? Women as their own worst . . .

The vote is 2 to 2 to 1. A hung jury. They'll have to go back and interview more people, and since (as it happens) the search is for a position in your field, imagine further that a colleague gives you the list of the original pool of candidates. The colleague requests your input *informal—drywall flies don't get an actual . . . voice.*

———

Statistically-speaking, it is the case that white, middle-class, heterosexual women have been the primary beneficiaries of affirmative action (and upper-middle-class women have had an extra bit of edge). In recent years, there has been a pandemic of appointments of white women to deanships and presidencies.

It's also often said about white women that of all marginalized groups, mine—white, hetero, middle- and lower-middle-class—has been the most complicit in our own oppression. It's been said that it's the white part that gets us. That white privilege thing. The whiteness allows us just enough power to be invested in the system— which motivates us to help maintain the system. Class matters, as well. The middle classes have just enough access to assets to think that if we just work hard enough—within the system—we'll end up with more. White middle classes end up power-blind, their women well-high-heeled—most all of them working for The Man. That One Percent of the population that Owns It All.

I've been around just long enough to watch the cooptation of white women manifest in academia. It's an old trick. Want to get rid of the union? Hire workers into some sort of management position. Give them just enough status so they'd wince if they lost it. And *voilà*: you've got yourself a company girl. You got yourself a female dean who, yeah—she won't fight you. She won't unify the faculty to work against you. She'll absorb all those budget cuts and close down the philosophy department for you. Sure. No prob.

Affirmative action is no longer affirmative action. It's absorption of dissensus. It's corroborative comportment.

That said, affirmative action's all we've got. Hell. How do you think *I* got here?

Where am I again?

———

The hung job search. *You light upon a male name.* This guy's smart. In fact, he's a former student of another guy who teaches in the program. Till now, this other guy's been uninvolved in the search. He's absented himself. Just didn't come to the meetings, the interviews, the dinners. Saw none of the previous *recall: female* candidates. Tenured faculty can get away with that, and from what I now know about how hard junior faculty work, I figure he deserves the break. *But he selects* this *search to take a break on. The search for a* woman. *And now that that's "failed"—chicks done in by the very chick who wanted a chick—NOW he wants in.* The male candidate, his former student *boys will be boys, when they're with boys* has published an unusual and ambitious book. And *and this is why I, a girl, know about him* he's edited an anthology of writing by women.

———

I don't believe that a man can be a feminist *per se*—experientially— but on paper at least this guy is clearly anti-sexist.

———

I anticipate an elitist audience.

———

I invite you to imagine, but not to *identify.* Not to sympathize. Not to *relate.*

My experience *an imagined site* differs from yours, even if you feel you relate to my stories. I tell the tales to illuminate that difference. That Gap. That Cowan's Gap, embraced by that bastion of impervious Pennsylvania poverty, of incestuous isolation. I defend the opening of my gap, of my opening—I defend my "no-no place," as a girlfriend calls her cunt.

So.

You think you fucked me off the board? You think I'll keep my fucking mouth shut? You think I'm so entirely implicated by my participation in this mess *stupid, stupid broad, they're thinking* that I won't yank open this kisser and blow?

You think I haven't been called *dumb* before?

— — —

Hung job. One of the men returns to the fray and reluctantly agrees that they should abandon the original *sexed* intention of the search. He argues for interviewing the male candidate. The new face in the crowd, the candidate's former teacher, attends the meeting. And against the strong wishes of the program director, who continues to insist that they should interview only women *I'm with ya, lady, but can't ya find one that might rock-n-roll the boat? just a little?* the committee agrees to interview the male candidate.

The candidate does smashingly well. He's smart, funny, personable. His work is interesting. It's an open and shut case. But the follow-up meeting does not go well. They vote to hire the guy but the director objects strongly—so strongly, in fact, that she tries to block the progress of the hire by going to the dean to request an EEOP review by the affirmative action officer.

The fight goes upstairs and backstage. Who *knows* what the fuck is going on. It's waaaaay above my pay grade. *Grades not yet posted.* But can you—

———

Imagine?

———

Check this out: a guy I admire (BFG who does interesting work) is editing a journal of experimental writing—challenging stuff, intellectually committed, primarily artistic critiques of the power associated with the social problem known as *meaning*. Most of the writers he publishes are men. He knows this is not good. He comes to me, asks me to round up some suitable manuscripts by women. I go to my acquaintances and ask for some. I choose a few manuscripts that would, I think, fit with what the men in his pages are doing. He reads them and says he doesn't like any. I ask what he doesn't like. He says the writing style is—

—wait for it—

Flaccid.

Yeah. He actually uses a term most often associated with a penis to denigrate writing by a woman.

I'm forced to return to my associates and report that things didn't work out—sorry to have troubled them *I really am.*

Then check this out: a woman whose journal of women's writing I admire (she's neither big nor famous nor, obviously, a guy—in fact, she's a [gasp] lesbian) says she wants to expand the types of writing she publishes. She asks me to round up some manuscripts that push the envelope, challenge the reader more. I go to my acquaintances and (see above). The editor reads and says she doesn't (etc.). I ask what she doesn't like. The editor says the writing style is too—

—wait for it—

Masculinist.

Is this the fun part? Are we having fun yet?

There's no emotional core, no moral center—it's doing that show-offy icky guy thing where it's smarter than the reader—it's counter-intuitive. It doesn't make . . . *sense!* How can you address oppression when you won't even make . . . *sense?*

But, I say, the standardization of language is, among other things, a masculinist—a patriarchal—victory. Language is how we know ourselves, it limits *and enables, yes* our capacity to envision change. Challenge language, challenge the way our society makes meaning *that "sense" thing you're so hung up on* and you're challenging those limitations. You're asserting a radical revisioning of yourself, selves, the self.

But I don't understand it! the editor replies.

I'm forced to return to my associates and (etc.).

———

Hang job. One evening the phone rings. It's the male candidate's former teacher, calling me.

Me.

He's never called me, ever. I'm a lowly adjunct. *A speck in the eye of that fly on the drywall.*

"May I," he says, "quote you, *as a feminist*, as having said that it's more important to get an anti-sexist man on the faculty than it is to have another female body on the faculty?"

Freeze. I'm *never* asked my opinion on anything regarding the policies of this university. In particular, this "colleague" of mine—really *not* my colleague, clearly—has never addressed me on *any* terms before.

This guy is really going to the mat for this guy, I think.

Almost simultaneously *phone still in hand* a question occurs to me *auto-investigation*. It's an unbecoming question and the moment it enters my head *in some not-actual but still-real way* I blush. It's the kind of question that would only enter the head of a . . . *careerist*! The sin I despise above all other sins! *Careerism*!

But *since we're telling the truth here*, there that thought sits, clanking around among my autoconflictual synapses.

To wit: *He wants to use me to help this guy. OK. But I wonder: would he ever go to these lengths to help me?*

Years have passed. I am able, consequently, to answer that question:

———

Alma mater. Mother tongue. In academe, two kinds of women are acceptable: the one that mommies you, and the one that does your dirty work.

Those are the options.

Same is pretty much true for people of color, gays, folks from the lower classes.

These latter seem to do extra well in the dirty-work department.

———

I'm not sure whether activists understand how affirmative action is now being used by The One Percents. We need to move from a practice that treats *race class gender* as individual Maypoles, and toward a practice that views all kinds of oppression as strands hanging from a pole cemented in the same foundation. We need a jackhammer to cut through the cement. What our institutions now require is intellectual, aesthetic, and perspectival diversity, an end to cooptation and assimilation as totalizing assurances of *no boat-rocking, no bait-eating.*

And *think*, just *think*, about how *implicated* our educational institutions *are* in that patriarchal cement. *Think* ABC. The top twenty private schools ($143,000/student). The institutions are the *sand* in the cement.

How do you, a prof, a student, a dean, a member of the institution—how do you, part of the sand in the cement, bust through *the very thing that comprises you?*

How does the foundation bulldoze the foundation?

Understand?

Understand?

———

Hand job. *Freeze.* I have to decide, on my toes and fast, whether I will be used in this way. Am I willing to stand by my principles and dismiss the anti-feminist, anti-intellectual *flaccid* female body (qualified as female merely by virtue of the presence of titsandass), in favor of the anti-sexist, anti-stupid *rockin'* penile body? Am I willing to be used, instrumentally, toward a set of institutional ends different, ultimately, from my own? Am I willing to be used by the old-boy network, which just *happens* in this event *strange bedfellows* to support my own ideal as well?

That is, is this a *gang* rape? Would allowing myself to be used in this manner produce the same results as fucking myself off the board?

Will I put my theories into practice, even if it could mean fucking myself? Will I stand by my principles?

Is it even OK to have principles—snob! That unmuffled white-ness, the guy next door on the stoop, blackness present but upstage left, dumb bunny choking out browngreen mountain—*how did I get here from there?* That quarry, that gap needing filled, that quarry the source—

Apropos of little, I'll take this *this!* opportunity *at this late date!* to add: A long, long time ago, when I was getting divorced and tell-ing my husband take-the-house-just-get-me-outta-here, my father said to me, "If someone's going to *fuck* you, you don't have to bend *over*."

Imagine me in my tarty red dress at the top of the stairs. Where shall I go, what shall I do, what shall I say?

In my hand, at my ear, a bad connection.

It's the twenty-first century (they say). The past is the past (they say).

I anticipate a racist, sexist and elitist audience, because I too am all of those things, and more. Or less.

"Sure," I say. "You can quote me."

SELECTED DALKEY ARCHIVE PAPERBACKS

FOR A FULL LIST OF PUBLICATIONS, VISIT:
www.dalkeyarchive.com